The COMPLETE ADOPTION & FERTILITY LEGAL GUIDE

Brette McWhorter Sember
Attorney at Law

SPHINX® PUBLISHING
AN IMPRINT OF SOURCEBOOKS, INC.®
NAPERVILLE, ILLINOIS
www.SphinxLegal.com

Copyright © 2004 by Brette McWhorter Sember
Cover and internal design © 2004 by Sourcebooks, Inc.®
Cover images © 2004 Taxi and Photodisc
Sourcebooks and the colophon are registered trademarks of Sourcebooks, Inc.®

First Edition, 2004

Published by: **Sphinx® Publishing, An Imprint of Sourcebooks, Inc.®**

<u>Naperville Office</u>
P.O. Box 4410
Naperville, Illinois 60567-4410
630-961-3900
Fax: 630-961-2168
www.sourcebooks.com
www.SphinxLegal.com/Sphinx

This publication is designed to provide accurate and authoritative information in regard to the subject matter covered. It is sold with the understanding that the publisher is not engaged in rendering legal, accounting, or other professional service. If legal advice or other expert assistance is required, the services of a competent professional person should be sought.
From a Declaration of Principles Jointly Adopted by a Committee of the American Bar Association and a Committee of Publishers and Associations

This product is not a substitute for legal advice.
Disclaimer required by Texas statutes.

Library of Congress Cataloging-in-Publication Data
Sember, Brette McWhorter, 1968-
  The complete adoption & fertility legal guide / by Brette McWhorter Sember.
    p. cm.
  Includes index.
  ISBN 1-57248-373-3 (alk. paper)
  1. Adoption--Law and legislation--United States--Popular works. 2. Human reproductive technology--Law and legislation--United States--Popular works. I. Title: Complete adoption and fertility legal guide. II. Title.
KF545.Z9S46 2004
346.7301'78--dc22
                          2004001920

Printed and bound in the United States of America.

BG — 10 9 8 7 6 5 4 3 2 1

Contents

Acknowledgement

This book is dedicated to my own two beautiful children who came to us after struggles with infertility. They are my joy. My thanks, as always, goes to my husband who supports me in all of my projects and makes me laugh and see the light in the world. I would also like to thank my own wonderful doctor, Dr. Maria Corigliano, who not only helped us conceive our children, but brought them both into the world with love and skill.

Introduction

So you want to have a family. There are many ways to create a family. In fact, there are more options available now than ever before. Singles or couples who want to become parents can choose one of the many kinds of adoption—stepparent, domestic agency adoption, international adoption, or independent adoption. Rapid advancements in reproductive technology have created many possibilities for parents who want to raise a child that is genetically linked to them. These new technologies, such as insemination, surrogacy, embryo adoption, egg donation, and evolving possibilities like cloning or nuclear transfer, allow parents to be connected to a baby from conception.

This book is your guide through the many family-building options available. Some people begin building a family with certain ideas about what choices they will consider, while others are unsure of what their options are and how they work. Whether you have a few distinct possibilities you are considering or whether you are still exploring all the options, this book helps you understand how each process or procedure works and explains how to make a child part of your family. This book takes a careful look at the legal procedures and requirements involved in family-building options and helps you understand what steps are necessary to make the child of your heart your legal child.

It is important to note that while this book strives to give you up-to-date legal information, laws are constantly changing. It is essential that you check with an attorney so you can get the most up-to-date information. It is also important to talk with an attorney so you can get personal legal advice based on your individual circumstances.

This book also helps you consider what you are and are not comfortable with and helps you evaluate the options. The book is filled with links to more information available online and an extensive resource list that will help you find books, magazines, organizations, and websites that can offer more information and answer questions.

Section I focuses on adoption, from the legal process to the many different adoption possibilities. Chapter 1 guides you through the adoption process and explains how adoption works, while Chapter 2 discusses the many options and considerations that are part of the adoption process. The legal procedures and the process you must go through to become an adoptive parent will be covered in Chapter 3. Chapter 4 explains stepparent, or second-parent, adoptions. Chapter 5 looks at kinship adoptions, in which a child is adopted by a relative, such as a grandparent or aunt. Chapter 6 examines adoption through a domestic agency, then Chapter 7 deals with international adoption.

Chapter 8 discusses independent (or parent-initiated) adoption when the adoptive parents locate a birth mother without the help of an agency. Chapter 9 explains the adoption of an adult by another adult. Chapter 10 focuses on the ever more commonplace single-parent adoption. Chapter 11 deals with same-sex couple adoption. Chapter 12 discusses how to cope with adoption and handle the bumps along the road, and Chapter 13 is about raising an adoptive child.

Section II deals with assisted reproduction. Chapter 14 helps you understand and evaluate reproductive technology and make informed choices and decisions that are right for you. Chapter 15 focuses on insemination, or sperm donation, and some of the issues that surround the use of donor sperm. Chapter 16 looks at egg donation, while Chapter 17 discusses embryo donation, also known as embryo adoption. Chapter 18 talks about the costly and controversial assisted reproductive treatment of surrogacy.

Chapter 19 examines emerging technologies such as cloning. Cryopreservation, or the freezing of eggs, sperm, and embryos, is the focus of Chapter 20. Finally, Chapter 21 discusses the issues involved in raising a child who was created using assisted reproductive technologies.

The goal of this book is to present you with information so that you can make an educated choice about how you would like to become a parent. Many couples or singles approach family building with the certainty that they want to use assisted reproduction and then later change their minds and consider adoption. The opposite also happens—prospective parents choose adoption, but then change their minds and use assisted reproduction. This book will guide you through all the choices and help you no matter what path you decide to pursue, now or in the future.

Building a family is one of the most important decisions you will make in your life. This book will help you as you consider and select the avenue that will work best for you.

Section I
Adoption

Chapter 1

Understanding Adoption

Adoption is a way to create a family outside of biological means. Children who are adopted are children of their families just as much as biological children. In recent years, adoption has become less of a secret and more of a celebrated route to parenthood. If you are considering adoption, it is important to first understand some of the general rules.

Legal Effects

When a child is adopted, the birth parents' legal ties to the child are completely severed. The child no longer has any legal connection to these parents. The adoptive parents become the child's legal parents. A new birth certificate is issued with their names listed as the parents. An adopted child has the exact same rights as a couple's biological child. Adopted children have the right to:

+ inherit from their adoptive parent(s) and adoptive families;
+ take their parents' last name(s);
+ collect benefits (such as social security) through their parent(s); and,
+ rely on their parent(s) for support.

Additionally, should a child's adoptive parents ever divorce, custody, and visitation will be decided in the same way as it would for biological children. Being adopted has no impact on custody and visitation since an adopted child is legally no different than a child that is born to a couple. Even if the child is the biological child of one parent and is then adopted by the other parent, both parents have the same rights.

Birth Parents' Rights and Roles

When a child is born to a woman, she is legally the child's mother, unless and until a court issues an order stating otherwise. Birth fathers' rights are a little more slippery, simply because the identity of a child's biological father is not always obvious. If a woman is married when she gives birth, her husband is the legal father of the child, unless it is proven otherwise. If a woman is unmarried, a man can admit to being the father (by signing documents such as an *admission of paternity* or through what is called the *putative father registry*) or a court can issue an order determining paternity based on DNA testing.

When a child is adopted, both birth parents must *consent* to the adoption (unless the birth father is unknown or cannot be located). The adoption process affords both birth parents a period of time to change their minds about the adoption once the process is in motion. (See Chapter 3 for more information.)

Once the adoption process is finalized, the birth parents have no further legal rights to the child. They can never come back and decide they have changed their minds and want custody, and they do not have any right to see or spend time with the child. There are cases where birth parents later challenge an adoption, but this is not the norm and only occurs when there is some kind of abnormality or problem in the way the adoption process was handled (for example, if one of the birth parents was not properly notified). It is important to understand that in most states, the birth parents have a period of time after the birth during which they can reconsider their consent to the adoption. This is not overturning the adoption; the adoption simply is not legal until this time period has ended.

Extended Birth Family

Adoption also severs the child's legal ties to the birth parents' families—grandparents, aunts, uncles, cousins, and so on. The child is no longer legally related to these people, which means these people have no claim to visitation with the child. There are also no longer any inheritance rights. For example, if a grandmother leaves everything to be divided equally among her grandchildren, a child who was placed for adoption with another family no longer qualifies as one of her grandchildren.

It is important to understand that adoption severs not only the rights of the birth family, but also their connection to the child. An adoption takes a child out of one family unit and places him or her into another. It is a complete and absolute substitution.

In some instances, however, a birth family continues to have contact with the child. It is becoming more common for a child to continue to have contact not only with birth parents, but also birth families. Despite the adoption, these people are a part of a child's history and even though the law changes their legal relationship, it is possible for them to continue to know each other. Often this is considered the healthiest way for an adoption to happen. You can change what a birth certificate says, but you cannot change a child's feelings. Continuing these family bonds can be important for older children who are adopted. This has to be done the right way, with the proper safeguards, so the child is not confused. (See Chapter 13 for more information.)

Legal Process

It is important to remember that the legal process is separate from the process you will go through to find a child to adopt. Finding a child can take much longer and can involve choosing an agency, finding a birth mother on your own, or dealing with the requirements of the foreign country your child will come from. (See Chapter 6 for information about agencies; Chapter 8 about independent adoptions; and Chapter 7 about international adoptions.)

The *legal process* for adoption follows the same general path whether your adoption is a single-parent adoption, second-parent adoption, agency adoption, private adoption, or international adoption. The major components of the process include:

- ✦ a background check, where prospective parents are fingerprinted and have their backgrounds checked for criminal records;
- ✦ a home study, in which a social worker meets with the prospective parents and sees their home;
- ✦ the birth parents' consent to the adoption; and,
- ✦ the actual court procedure in which documents are submitted, reviewed, and the adoption is approved.

The legal process itself can take six months to a year. (See Chapter 3 for more information about the specific legal processes involved in adoption.)

Making the Decision to Adopt

If you are considering adopting through an agency, internationally, or directly through a private birth mother, consider joining an adoption support group. (See Appendix A for more information.) These groups can provide practical information, contact information, support, and advice. Talking to other parents who have adopted or who are going through the adoption process will provide you with a clear perspective on how the process works and how it affects parents.

A support group is an excellent way to make connections, get information, hear other people's experiences, and consider new approaches. For example, you might only be considering an agency adoption, but through a support group you might learn of a birth mother interested in independent adoption. You will meet other couples seeking to adopt, as well as families that have successfully adopted. You may also meet attorneys and other adoption professionals who can assist you with your adoption journey.

> Locate an adoption group in your area using this resource: **www.adoptiointriad.org/support/index.htm**

If you are considering a second-parent adoption, the decision process is a bit different since the child is already in your life. You are now confronting a legal decision, not a family forming-decision. This is a decision you must make with your partner or spouse and often with the child's input as well. Second-parent adoptions must also consider the child's other parent, if he or she is alive, since his or her consent will be necessary.

Some people come to the adoption process after unsuccessfully attempting to conceive a child themselves, with or without *assisted reproduction treatments*. Others simply know that adoption is the way for them to create or add to a family. No matter what your reasons are, be sure they make sense to you and work for your family. Choosing between adopting and using infertility treatments can be a difficult one. Help weighing out your options and making a decision can be found later in this book. (See Chapter 14 for more information.)

It is possible, and perfectly acceptable, to pursue adoption while undergoing infertility treatment, also called *assisted reproductive treat-*

ment, such as IVF, GIFT, and other procedures. (See Chapter 14 for more information about these options.) An adoption agency will not turn you away, but it may make them think twice about whether you would choose not to complete the adoption should you become pregnant. Many couples feel that adoption and assisted reproduction is an either/or proposition, when in fact many couples do explore and pursue both choices simultaneously. Because both processes can be long, it may make sense to consider both.

> If you are considering adoption, take an adoption self-assessment to help you and your partner (if any) get a clear sense as to how you feel about the many choices available. One is available at:
>
> **http://adoption.about.com/library/adopt/blselfeval.htm**

Preparing for the Adoption Rollercoaster

No matter what kind of adoption you are considering or have selected, it is likely that the process will be emotional. Choosing to create a family is one of the most private decisions, yet when you choose to do so through adoption, suddenly there are social workers, lawyers, adoption case managers, and judges scrutinizing you, your life, your decision, your abilities, and your desirability. It can be disconcerting and frustrating to know that the future of your family is in large part in the hands of these strangers. It also can be frustrating to realize that people who have biological children can have them without any approval or screening (and sometimes with little thought), but someone who desperately wants a child and wishes to adopt must go through an intrusive process.

> Joining an adoption support group is an excellent way to get through the waiting. Consider joining an online group, such as:
>
> **www.adoptioncommunity.com**

Some adoption processes take longer and can be more difficult than others. If you are hoping to adopt a newborn in the United States, you may realize that finding a birth mother is a long and difficult process. If you are planning a second-parent adoption, you might be frustrated by the hoops that must be jumped through to make legal something that seems and feels obvious to you.

While waiting to adopt, it is important to have patience. Do everything you can to make the paperwork go smoothly. Never lose your belief that you will find your child.

While none of the adoption processes are as simple as sperm meeting egg, they are not as scary and drawn out as some people expect. Remember that the reward at the end is a child. That will make everything feel worthwhile.

Preparing for the Future

When you decide to adopt, your decision affects not only you and your partner, if you have one, but also your entire extended family. It also, of course, affects the child you bring into your family. Adoption is a decision that you may make today, but will impact the long term future in many ways. When making the decision, it is important to consider how it will affect you and your family in the long term.

You must also give some thought to how your decision will affect the child you adopt. The type of adoption you choose will have an impact on your child. If you use an agency adoption, your child will probably grow up with little or no contact with his or her birth parents. If you use independent adoption, it is likely your child will have some sort of contact with, or at least will know how to contact, his or her birth parents. International adoption usually completely rules out any hope of your child having any contact with the birth parents. The results of any of these paths can have a long-term impact on you and your child, so it is important to consider every angle as you are making your decision.

Chapter 2

Adoption Decisions

Once you have chosen to adopt, you will find that there are many more decisions ahead of you. You must choose:

+ the type of adoption you are interested in;
+ the people who will help you; and,
+ what kind of relationship you want to have with the birth parents in the future.

Open versus Closed Adoption

Adoptions used to be done in complete secrecy, with even the child being kept in the dark. Today, things have changed and most people are more honest about adoptions. Most adoptive children now grow up understanding that they were adopted. This concept of an *open adoption* is one in which the adoptive and birth parents have some contact (that can vary greatly) and the child knows that he or she is adopted. The child may even know or have contact with the birth parents.

The degree of contact can range from minimal to very involved. For example, some adoptive parents see the birth mother frequently during the pregnancy, attend the birth, and continue to see her and have contact with her throughout the child's life. In other situations, an open adoption can mean that the adoptive parents meet the birth mother once, learn her first name, and obtain copies of her family medical history. A middle road alternative includes some meetings or contact during pregnancy and photos and letters exchanged occasionally throughout the child's life.

The type of adoption you pursue will affect how open it is to some degree. *International adoptions* provide no contact with birth parents; *private adoptions* can be some of the most open; and, *domestic agency adoptions* can vary greatly depending on the agency's policies, your wishes, and the birth mother's wishes.

> Read a sample open adoption agreement online at:
> **http://public.findlaw.com/nllg/forms/oo6.html**

Choosing an open or closed adoption depends on your personal feelings. It is important to understand that your adoption will not be specified as an open one or a closed one in your adoption papers. The court cannot require you to send photos to the birth mother, but it cannot prevent you from having a relationship with her either. As far as the court is concerned, the adoptive parents become the legal parents and the birth parents have no further rights once the adoption is completed. The adoption legal process completely ends the birth parents' legal rights, but anything you choose to do from that point is up to you. It is important to realize that some birth mothers will not agree to the adoption if they do not feel you have made a commitment to the level of openness (or closure) they are seeking.

> For more information about open adoption, contact the
> *American Association of Open Adoption Agencies* at:
> **www.openadoption.org**

An important consideration in open adoption is how very real the baby and birth mother can be to you as you are waiting for the birth. This can be wonderful, because in a way you are included in the pregnancy process. It can also be heartbreaking if the birth mother ultimately decides not to go through with the adoption. Because you are so heavily invested in the situation and because the baby and birth mother are so much a part of you life, it can be emotionally very difficult to cope if the adoption is not completed.

An open adoption can place more pressure on the adoptive parents. They must meet and be interviewed by the agency, the social worker who does the home study, and sometimes by the birth mother. It can be very difficult to sit in a room with a woman who is carrying what might be your baby and try to measure up to whatever standards she is using.

Some adoptive parents find that the relationship they carry on with the birth mother during the pregnancy can be emotionally draining. Some people never feel quite sure how involved to get, what kind of help to offer, or even what to say at certain times. Your agency can help guide you through this process for the most part, but it is something to consider.

Finally, some adoptive parents simply do not want the specter of the birth mother intruding on their lives. They do not want to meet or interact with her or think too much about her role or her connection to the baby once that child becomes theirs. Many adoptive parents feel she will exert some kind of emotional influence over the child and always be the *real* mother. These are individual decisions you must make on your own. As always, an adoption support group can help you through these thought processes and decisions.

Domestic versus International Adoption

Choosing between adopting a child within the United States or from another country is a common dilemma faced by potential adoptive parents. With domestic adoptions, it is generally easier to adopt a younger and possibly more healthy child than it is to adopt from another country. However, international adoptions tend to be quicker and can be less costly.

The following two lists identify the pros and cons to each option. Choose the path that is most comfortable for you and your family.

Information to help you consider domestic versus international adoption is available at:

www.adoptall.com/intguide.html

Domestic Adoption

Pros:

- ✦ It is easier to adopt a newborn.
- ✦ The child is usually healthy and developmental delays are limited.
- ✦ You can obtain complete medical records for the baby.
- ✦ You can obtain complete family medical history.
- ✦ Everything is conducted in English.
- ✦ You may be able to meet or have contact with the birth parents.
- ✦ The agency you are working with may be the one the child is placed through (which can simplify things).
- ✦ As complicated as the adoption process is, it is done only using the laws of this country and the requirements are very clear.

Cons:

- ✦ These adoptions generally take a year or longer.
- ✦ You may have to wait longer to get a newborn.
- ✦ You may have to deal with a birth mother who could change her mind after the baby is born.
- ✦ Your child may be able to one day meet and know the birth parents.
- ✦ You may have to meet a birth mother's selection criteria.

International Adoption

Pros:

- ✦ These adoptions generally happen more quickly.
- ✦ There is no shortage of children available.
- ✦ The cost of the adoption is usually less than with domestic adoption.
- ✦ You gain not only a child but an entire culture that becomes part of your family.

Cons:

- ✦ The child you adopt is usually no younger than 3 or 4 months old (newborns are not available because of the way the process works).
- ✦ Children may not be in good health and may have developmental delays.
- ✦ You may get little or no medical information about your child or his or her family.
- ✦ You will have the added expense of travel.
- ✦ The red tape you may need to deal with in your child's country of origin may be extensive.

Agency versus Private Adoption

An *agency adoption* is one in which you work with an agency that will locate a child for you to adopt and provides most, if not all, the related services. In a *private adoption*, you locate a birth mother on your own—through adoption attorneys, adoption facilitators, or on your own (often through word of mouth or by placing newspaper ads). However, many adoptive parents who do private adoptions use an agency to handle the adoption once the birth mother is located.

One of the most comprehensive and helpful resources available to parents seeking to adopt is the *National Adoption Information Clearinghouse.* Its website is almost certain to provide answers to almost any question you have. Find it at:
http://naic.acf.hhs.gov

Some agencies can be difficult to work with, but when pursuing a private adoption, the entire process can be even more complicated. With each method having its own set of pros and cons, you must decide which one best suits your situation. Review the two lists on the following pages to help in your decision-making.

Agency Adoption

Pros:

+ The agency locates the child and does the legwork.
+ The agency provides the social worker for the home study.
+ The agency provides counseling and services.
+ The agency is in charge of the adoption and moving it along.
+ A good agency has plenty of children to adopt.
+ The agency can help manage your relationship with the birth parents.
+ The agency screens birth parents and usually chooses those less likely to change their minds.
+ The search time may be shorter since the agency already has a network set up to locate birth mothers.
+ The agency screens the adoptive parents and chooses those that the birth parents will not object to.

Cons:

+ The agency is in charge and things move at their pace, not yours.
+ The agency can screen you out if they feel you are not desirable.
+ You have no actual control over the process.
+ You must pay agency fees in addition to other adoption expenses.

Private Adoptions

Pros:

- ✦ You have control of the situation.
- ✦ You can develop the kind of relationship with the birth mother that feels right to you.
- ✦ You decide the pace at which the process moves.
- ✦ You can personally find and select a birth mother.
- ✦ You have more information about the birth parents.
- ✦ There are fewer people involved.
- ✦ There are no agency fees.
- ✦ You can immediately begin to bond with the child and can have extensive contact with the birth mother during the pregnancy.

Cons:

- ✦ The process can be riskier, with the birth mother more likely to change her mind.
- ✦ You may need to spend a lot of time searching or advertising for birth mothers.
- ✦ You do not have as many professionals guiding you and supporting you.
- ✦ You are responsible for understanding the laws of your state or finding an attorney to guide you as you look for birth mothers.
- ✦ The costs are more unpredictable.
- ✦ You cannot select the gender of the child—whatever your birth mother has, you get.
- ✦ It can be more stressful than going through an agency.

Finding and Choosing an Agency

If you choose to work with an agency to adopt, it will be important to take some time to interview several agencies and choose the one that you are most comfortable with and confident in. You will be paying the agency a lot of money and you want to make sure that you get the results you want.

If you are seeking to do an international adoption or a domestic adoption (which is not a private adoption or a second-parent adoption) you will have to use an agency. Agencies can be profit or nonprofit, but both still charge fees. Agencies may be public (run by the state) or private (run by a private company). Agencies can also be religious or nonsectarian, but it is important to know that most religious-based agencies do not require adoptive parents to be members of that religion.

An agency cannot reject you because of race or religion. However, marital status can be used as a determining factor, as can sexual orientation.

The best way to locate an agency is by word of mouth, through adoption support groups, or through people you know who have used an agency successfully. Once you have a few names of agencies to consider, make an initial phone call and request information by mail. If the agency has a website, be sure to visit it. Many agencies provide informational meetings you can attend to learn more about the agency as well as the adoption process. Do not sign up with any agency before you have time to ask questions, compare it to others, and think about the decision. Ask about informational meetings and be sure to attend them. Ask questions and be observant. If you still feel the agency is a possibility, schedule an interview and use the questionnaire beginning on page 26 to evaluate and record responses.

One thing you will need to get a clear picture of is the agency's fee. The agency will collect fees to cover the home study, application, birth mother's expenses (if it is a domestic adoption), and other costs. Some agencies will clearly enunciate these separate amounts for you. Be wary of an agency that lumps total costs together and will not provide a break down.

Call your state's agency that licenses and monitors adoption agencies (your social services or family and children department) and ask for information about the adoption agency, including its history and any complaints that have been filed against it. Ask to speak to an adoption specialist in the department and question the agency's reputation.

The average length of time for an adoption should be under two years. If an agency has a longer average, you may want to go somewhere else.

When you have chosen an agency, make sure you get everything in writing so there can be no confusion or dispute. You will need to sign a contract with the agency that will spell out the fees, procedures, and responsibilities. (See Chapters 6 and 7 for more information about evaluating agencies.)

Finding and Choosing an Attorney

No matter what type of adoption you choose to pursue, you will need an attorney to represent you. It is important to select an attorney who is experienced in handling adoptions. If you have an attorney you have used for other matters, ask him or her for a referral. Ask members of your adoption support group for referrals. You can also call your state or city bar association and ask for a referral.

Once you have some attorneys to consider, schedule a free consultation. Use the *Attorney Questionnaire* at the end of the chapter to help you evaluate the attorney. Make sure you get a clear picture of the attorney's fees. If you are seeking a private adoption, you will need to find out if the attorney is able to help you locate birth mothers or if he or she will only handle the legal paperwork.

Expect attorney fees to range from $2000 to $7000, depending on the type of adoption and where you live. Avoid attorneys who seek *contingency fees* (paid only if they accomplish certain things such as finding a child for you to adopt). This can motivate an attorney to use nonethical means to find a child for you to adopt. Make sure that when you do select an attorney, that your agreement with him or her is in writing and is in the form of a retainer agreement or retainer letter.

For a referral to an attorney, contact:
American Academy of Adoption Attorneys
P.O. Box 33053
Washington, DC 20033
202-832-2222
www.adoptionattorneys.org

Facilitators

Adoption *facilitators* are professionals who locate birth mothers for adoptive parents. They can play an ongoing role throughout the adoption process and take on a coordinating position similar to that an agency plays. Be aware that many states do not permit the use of adoption facilitators. Some states do permit facilitators to operate, but do not license or regulate them. (California does license facilitators.) Be sure to talk to your attorney about the legalities of using a facilitator. Also, be certain to check references and backgrounds of any facilitators you consider. Do not work with anyone without a contract and make sure that your attorney approves the contract.

The following states do not permit paid adoption facilitators:
+ Colorado
+ Florida
+ Georgia
+ Kentucky
+ Maryland
+ Missouri
+ New Jersey
+ New York
+ Oklahoma
+ Oregon
+ Tennessee
+ Virginia
+ West Virginia

It is important to distinguish between paid and unpaid facilitators. Unpaid facilitators are the way many adoptions happen. A minister, doctor, therapist, or nurse might work with a woman who is pregnant and help her find an agency or an adoptive family. These facilitators are doing nothing wrong. Many states object to *paid* facilitators. Part of the problem is that these kinds of facilitators fall outside the specific requirements that states place on adoption agencies and can operate on their own. There may come a time when all states will license, regulate, and allow facilitators, but for now, you must be very clear about what your state permits and does not permit.

For more information on state laws about facilitators and other adoption laws, visit:

www.theadoptionguide.com

If you can use a facilitator, the advantage is that the relationship is more personal than with an agency. He or she personally (for the most part) handles the details of your adoption and is personally accountable to you. The downside is that in most states, a facilitator is not licensed or regulated and operates completely on his or her own, with no safeguards for adoptive families and no required training.

Affording Adoption

When considering adoption, many people are taken aback by the costs involved. It can be particularly difficult to accept the costs if you are adopting a special needs child. However, affording adoption can be easier than you think. Once you have adopted a child, you are eligible for tax credit to reimburse you for expenses. (See Chapter 3 for more information.) Many employers offer adoption cost partial reimbursement programs.

You may also wish to consider purchasing *adoption insurance*. It will reimburse you for expenses if a planned adoption does not take place. Adoption insurance can be difficult to locate, but one source is MBO Insurance Brokers in Menlo Park, California (800-833-7337). You might also talk to an insurance broker in your area.

For more information about adoption insurance, contact:
National Adoption Foundation
100 Mill Plain Rd.
Danbury, CT 06811
203-791-3811
www.nafadopt.org/default.asp

NOTE: *These types of insurance policies often only apply if you work with agencies or attorneys on the list approved by the insurance carrier.*

The National Adoption Foundation has $9 million in revolving loans available to adoptive parents. Some of these loans are unsecured loans, meaning you do not put up any security, such as a house, to guarantee the loan. They also offer home equity loans in which your home is used as security for the loan. The loans typically average $2500 and are financed through MBNA bank.

Adoption is expensive, but it is not completely out of reach for most families. If you are considering adoption, you may wish to create a separate bank account and start saving what you can to help pay for the costs. Look into the special adoption loans available or consider a home equity loan through your own bank. You might also consider letting family and friends know you are saving for adoption and ask for contributions to your fund instead of holiday or birthday gifts. (Any person can give up to $11,000 tax free per year to any other person as a gift.)

If you are planning to add a child to your family, you already know that the child will bring added expenses. The money you earn now will have to stretch further to accommodate a child's needs. You can make adoption affordable by beginning to act like parents now—take the money it would cost to raise a child each week or each month and set that aside to help pay for the adoption.

Another consideration is comparing adoption expenses with assisted reproduction treatment expenses. The cost of adopting a child may turn out to be a lot less than pursuing months of unsuccessful fertility treatments. This is a choice you must weigh on your own, since obviously money is not the only consideration when choosing how you will add a child to your family.

Agency Evaluation
Questionnaire

Name of Agency_____

Name of Contact Person_____

Date of Interview_____

Questions:

❏ Are you licensed in this state?_____

_____

❏ How long have you been in business?_____

_____

❏ Can you provide references?_____

_____

❏ Do you handle domestic or international adoptions?_____

    ❏ If both, which do you place more often?_____

    _____

❏ Can you place children from other states?_____

_____

❏ Do you have religious restrictions?_____

_____

❏ What other guidelines or restrictions do you have in place?

_____

_____

❏ What is your fee structure?_____

_____

    ❏ Can you provide a breakdown?_____

    ❏ When are the amounts due?_____

    ❏ What fees are not included in this?_____

    _____

❏ What is the average length of time for one of your adoptions?

_____

❏ How many placements do you make per year?_____

    ❏ How many in the last year?_____

❏ How many people are on your waiting list to adopt?_____

❏ Do you have infants available?_____

(continued)

❏ What is the average age of the children placed through your agency?_____

❏ What portion of fees are refundable if the adoption does not occur?_____

❏ Please explain your home study process._____

_____

   ❏ How long does it take?_____

_____

❏ Can you provide a list of approved social workers to use for the home study?_____

❏ Will you assist with a private adoption?_____

   ❏ What fees would apply?_____

_____

❏ How are your birth mothers located?_____

_____

❏ Who makes the placement decision—the agency or the birth mother?_____

   ❏ How is placement decided?_____

_____

❏ What is your position on open adoption?_____

_____

   ❏ What kind of relationship do you encourage or advise for birth parents and adoptive parents?_____

_____

❏ Do you provide counseling for birth and adoptive parents?

_____

   ❏ Are there additional fees for this?_____

   ❏ What is involved in the counseling process?_____

_____

❏ What medical history information is provided to adoptive parents about the birth parents?_____

_____

   ❏ Are birth mothers screened for HIV and other conditions?

_____

(continued)

❏ If potential adoptive parents turn down a birth mother, may they continue in the program and receive the next available placement?_____

_____

❏ If an adoption is not completed, can the expenses be transferred or rolled over to a new birth mother?_____

_____

❏ What other services does the agency provide?_____

_____

❏ What is your policy on divorce, singles, and families with biological children?_____

_____

❏ Do you have a grievance policy?_____

_____

   ❏ If so, how does it work?_____

   _____

   ❏ If not, how are problems resolved?_____

   _____

Attorney Evaluation
Questionnaire

Name of Firm_____

Name of Attorney_____

Date of Interview_____

Questions:

❏ How long have you practiced adoption law?_____

_____

❏ What states are you licensed in?_____

_____

❏ How many adoptions do you handle per year?_____

_____

❏ How many have you handled in the last six months?_____

_____

❏ Do you handle domestic or international adoptions or both?

_____

   ❏ What percent of your practice is made up of these two
   types?_____

❏ Do you handle private adoptions?_____

_____

   ❏ How many have you handled?_____

   _____

   ❏ What role do you take in the private adoption process?

   _____

❏ What are your fees?_____

_____

   ❏ Do you charge a flat fee or an hourly rate?_____

   _____

      ❏ What kind of payment schedule do you use?

      _____

❏ Can you recommend any agencies that you have worked with
in the past?_____

_____

❏ How long does the average adoption process take?_____

_____

Chapter 3

Adoption Procedures

While there are a variety of different types of adoption to consider and choose from, some things are common to all the choices. You will need a home study; you will need to understand the issues of consent and revocation of consent by birth parents; and, you will face a court procedure to finalize the adoption. This chapter provides an overview of these considerations and procedures. Later chapters will discuss specifics that apply to each different type of adoption.

Home Studies

A *home study* is an evaluation and investigation of prospective parents' histories, parenting abilities, home, lifestyle, and parenting abilities. Home studies are required in almost all adoptions, but in some states they may be waived for second-parent adoptions. (See Chapter 4 for more information.)

A home study is done by a licensed *social worker*. When working with an agency, the agency may have a list of social workers it works with or may have social workers who are employed by the agency. Make sure that the social worker you use is licensed in your state.

The home study is probably the most feared hurdle in the adoption process by many prospective parents. In reality, it is not nearly as terrifying as it may sound.

See a sample adoption home study online at:
www.1-800-homestudy.com/sample.html

A social worker will come to your home, meet you and your spouse (if you have one), and ask you questions about your background. These questions can cover information such as:

+ where you were born;
+ your family;
+ your education;
+ your job history;
+ any previous marriages;
+ any previous addresses;
+ any arrests or convictions; and,
+ other children you have.

The social worker will also ask questions about your lifestyle and personal life. These questions can cover topics including:

+ your employment schedule;
+ income;
+ friends and family you spend time with;
+ organizations you belong to;
+ pets;
+ religious beliefs;
+ hobbies and interests;
+ smoking, drinking, and drug use;
+ medical conditions;
+ infertility and any treatments you have undergone or are undergoing;
+ why you want to adopt;
+ how you plan to make room in your life for a child;
+ where the child will sleep;
+ child care plans;

◆ how you will discipline a child; and,

◆ how you will adjust your finances to include a child.

There is no right answer to any of these questions. The most important thing you can do is be honest. Dishonesty is the biggest mistake you can make because it will usually be discovered and then the social worker and agency will have to wonder why you lied or what else you were not honest about.

In general, the purpose of the questions is to find out if you have a stable lifestyle, if you would be able to raise a child, if you have a support network in place (*i.e.*, family and friends), if you are financially stable and can support a child, if your home is conducive to a child, and if you can emotionally handle being a parent. No parent is perfect, so no one is going to expect you to present a perfect picture of yourself.

You can prepare yourself for these questions by simply reading over the list of questions and thinking about what you might say. It is a mistake to prepare a script for yourself—to recite answers you have planned and memorized—but thinking through the questions in advance and coming up with some general ideas about how you will respond can make you feel more comfortable.

The social worker will want to see your home and will be particularly interested in where the child will sleep. Your home does not have to be spotless and it does not have to be childproofed. However, it is a good idea to show that you understand the basics of childproofing and explain how you will make the home safe for a child.

You may need to meet with the social worker more than once to cover all the information that is needed. Do not become overwhelmed by this process. Some prospective parents spend weeks repainting the house and decorating a nursery. Doing so may make you seem a little overanxious, but it is certainly nothing the social worker has not seen before. Your home should simply be relatively clean and neat. This is not a contest to decide who would be the best parent. The home study is simply a way of making sure you are decent people who are able to care for a child.

Additionally, you will be asked to write an autobiographical statement that will probably reiterate the information you provide verbally. This statement is brief—just a page or two—and should include information about why you want to adopt, as well as a brief history of your life. You will need to provide certified copies of birth and marriage certificates (as well as divorce decrees if applicable) and a medical report from your physician describing your health and explaining any conditions you have. You will also need written verification of your income (pay stubs or tax returns).

Another part of the home study is providing references—three to five people who know you well and can say nice things about you. This should include a variety of people, such as friends, neighbors, clergy, coworkers, and so on. They will be asked to provide letters explaining how they know you, how long they have known you, and why they believe you would make good adoptive parents.

Choose people who know you well. It would look strange to get a reference from someone who has only known you a short while. Select people that are themselves upstanding members of the community. It is always a good idea to include a reference from a minister, rabbi, or priest if you are involved in a church or temple. (It is ok if you are not religious and there is no need to join a church or temple just so you can get a letter of reference.)

In general, it is a good idea to choose people who have some kind of status—people with respected jobs, such as teachers, lawyers, business owners, and so on. While a good friend who is a hair stylist may know you well and have wonderful things to say about you, a letter from someone else who knows you well and has a more respected profession is probably going to look better. However, always remember to stick to people who know you well—that is more important than any status.

You will also need to be fingerprinted and/or have a criminal background check done. If your state requires fingerprints, you will be given a card or paperwork and be told to go to your local police station to be fingerprinted. A background check requires you to complete a form with your name, address, and Social Security number. This is then run through a computer to check for convictions, child abuse problems, or outstanding warrants.

If you have been arrested or convicted of a crime, all is not lost. The *Adoption and Safe Families Act* is a federal law that specifies which crimes states should screen for. Each state can opt out of these requirements and create their own, so it is important to check your state laws for specific information. In general, you are prohibited from adopting if you have been convicted (not just arrested) for:

crimes against children:
+ child abuse
+ child neglect

felonies consisting of:
+ spousal abuse
+ crime against a child (such as child pornography)
+ rape
+ sexual assault
+ homicide

felonies in the past five years consisting of:
+ physical assault
+ battery

drug related offenses.

Keep in mind, there is generally a separate fee for the home study (which can range from $700 to $2000). If you are working with an agency, this may not be included in the agency fees.

Once you have jumped through all the required hoops, the social worker will write up a report that describes you and includes a recommendation as to whether or not you should adopt. The entire home study process can take anywhere from a few weeks to a few months, depending on how quickly things can be scheduled.

Ask to receive a copy of the complete home study. The home study will be valid for either a year or eighteen months. Most adoptions can be completed within that time frame.

Consent

All adoptions involve some form of *consent*—agreement by the birth parents that the child should be adopted. If there are no living birth parents or the child was abandoned, then consent must be given by the state or country where the child is a resident. Consent is the biggest and most important hurdle to adoption. Procedures are in place to make sure birth parents are given adequate time to make their decision.

The type of consent required varies in each state. The birth parents must sign a document in which they consent to the adoption and agree to give up all their rights to the child. In many states, the birth parents must also appear before a judge and verbally agree to the consent. Some states have the birth mother file a paper with the court called a *petition of relinquishment*. The birth mother can only give consent after the birth of the child, while the birth father can consent before birth. The thinking is that birth mothers often feel different after they have given birth to and have seen their child. (See the chart on page 38 for complete details on consent laws.)

The birth mother must always provide consent to the adoption. The birth father must also provide consent, if *paternity* has been established. Paternity can be established through an *admission* by the father or through a court proceeding. Many states also have what is called a *putative father registry*. This is a place where a man can register if he believes he is the father of a child. Before a child is placed for adoption, the putative father registry must be searched. If someone has registered, paternity will be tested.

BIRTH FATHERS

Fathers' rights are an area of growing concern in the legal community. The problem with fathers' rights is that a birth father often does not know that he has fathered a child and the adoption happens without his knowledge or consent. The putative father registry helps with this issue, but does not completely alleviate it since if a man has no idea that a woman he was involved with became pregnant, he has no reason to register. Most men do not go and register every sexual encounter they have.

The *Baby Richard* case that occurred in Illinois is one many people think of when they think about the issue of fathers' rights. What many people do not understand about that case is that the birth mother lied to the birth father and told him the baby had died at birth, when instead she placed the baby for adoption. He later discovered the lie and eventually gained custody of the child who was, by that time, 4 years old. The birth mother also attempted to revoke her consent to the adoption. This case had components most cases do not—the marriage between the birth parents and the lie that was told.

Although the *Baby Richard* case is one that is unlikely to be repeated, it is a good example of why it is important to have consent from both birth parents whenever possible. In some instances that is not possible—and if your attorney is comfortable with the situation, then you should feel comfortable as well.

OLDER CHILDREN

In most states, older children that are adopted must give their consent. The age varies from state-to-state:

age 10:
- ✦ Alaska
- ✦ Arkansas
- ✦ Hawaii
- ✦ Maryland
- ✦ New Jersey
- ✦ New Mexico
- ✦ North Dakota

age 12:
- ✦ Arizona
- ✦ California
- ✦ Colorado
- ✦ Connecticut
- ✦ Florida
- ✦ Idaho
- ✦ Kentucky
- ✦ Massachusetts
- ✦ Montana
- ✦ New Hampshire
- ✦ North Carolina
- ✦ Ohio
- ✦ Oklahoma
- ✦ Pennsylvania
- ✦ South Dakota
- ✦ Texas
- ✦ Utah
- ✦ West Virginia

age 14:
- Alabama
- Delaware
- District of Columbia
- Georgia
- Illinois
- Indiana
- Iowa
- Kansas
- Maine
- Michigan
- Minnesota
- Mississippi
- Missouri
- Nebraska
- Nevada
- New York
- Oregon
- Rhode Island
- South Carolina
- Vermont
- Virginia
- Washington
- Wyoming

A child's consent is not required:
- Louisiana
- Tennessee
- Wisconsin

No Consent Needed

Consent is not needed if the birth parent has *abandoned* the child, had his or her rights *terminated* by the state (usually through an abuse or neglect proceeding in which the child is placed in foster care and then eventually freed up for adoption), is *dead*, or if there are *special circumstances*, such as failure of the parent to have contact with the child for a lengthy period of time. These situations normally occur when a child is in foster care and the state has terminated the parental rights. There are instances when a child can be placed for adoption by a birth mother and no consent will be needed from the birth father, if he has abandoned the child or had no contact with the child for a certain period of time, as specified in your state adoption laws.

When no consent is needed from the birth parents, the procedure seems as if it should go more quickly, but in reality it usually takes the same period of time. Adoptions are time consuming because of the amount of paperwork that must be processed about the adoptive parents and because many families are waiting to find a child to adopt. The consent process does not add that much time to the process. At the most it may add a month or two if there is an extended period after birth during which the birth mother can change her mind.

Notice

In some cases, the birth father may not be part of the child's life or may not be able to be located. In instances where this occurs, the court will allow *notice* to be given to him. This can include sending certified letters or court documents to his last known address or workplace or publishing a notice in a newspaper selected by the court. If the father does not respond, he is presumed to have waived his right to oppose the adoption. If notice is required in your adoption, your attorney will take careful steps to make sure it is done correctly. If notice is not given properly, the birth father could later come back and seek custody.

If notice is given properly and the birth father does not respond, his rights are terminated. Once parental rights are terminated, they can only be changed by showing that the proper procedure was not followed. If your state notice laws are carefully followed, there should not be problems with a birth father coming back later and trying to contest the adoption.

Timing of Consent

Birth fathers can give consent to adoption at any time. However, there are specific time frames in which a birth mother can give consent and have it be valid. This is usually only after the child is born. Alabama and Hawaii allow consent beforehand, but require a *reaffirmation* after the birth. There is usually a waiting period between the birth and when the birth mother's consent becomes final, and that can vary from twelve hours after the birth to fifteen days afterwards. (See Chapter 1 for more information about consent laws and timing.)

Consent Procedures

Birth parent consent can be done in writing (usually notarized) in some states. Other states require that it be done in court—either by appearing before the judge or by filing certain court papers. The birth parent must indicate that he or she understands the ramifications of what he or she is doing and willingly gives up all rights to the child.

The consent procedure is very simple when it occurs in court. The adoption case is scheduled for a court appearance. The birth mother appears and simply tells the court she consents to the adoption. The judge makes sure she understands exactly what she is agreeing to and that she is agreeing to it of her own volition. There is no trial or complicated hearing involved.

Revocation

Revocation is the withdrawal of consent by a birth parent. Everyone who is looking to adopt has heard horror stories about adoptions being revoked at the last minute. Revocation is actually difficult to do. A few states do not allow any revocation under any circumstances. Others permit revocation only if there has been fraud, coercion, or other factors that indicate that the birth parent did not have complete knowledge or free will at the time of the consent. A few states allow birth parents to change their minds for any reason within a certain time period.

If a birth mother revokes her consent, the adoption does not occur. Usually, if there is an agency involved, there will be last minute negotiations to try to complete the adoption, but by law, once a birth mother changes her mind, the adoptive family has no rights. The child is not theirs until the adoption is finalized and the adoption is not finalized without the completion of the consent.

While it is a sad thing to have happen, it is a possibility that all adoptive families must confront. The good news is that most birth mothers do not try to revoke their consent. To avoid a consent problem, it is important that the birth mother receive counseling during and after the pregnancy. It is also important that adoptive parents pursue only those adoptions that they have good feelings about and that seem likely to go through. If an adoption does fall through, you must know that it is not your fault and there is nothing you could have done to change the situation, as heartbreaking as it may be. You would not want to adopt a child knowing that you are taking him or her away from the birth mother against her will. Even if you believe that you can provide a better home for the child, you must accept the fact that the birth mother has the absolute right to keep her child if she so decides within the period of time allowed in your state. Once the court has finalized the adoption, there is no possibility that the adoption can be revoked. (Court proceedings are discussed later in this chapter.)

The following lists discuss when revocation is allowed and the time periods after consent for revocation in each state.

No revocation allowed unless fraud, duress, etc:

+ Arizona
+ California (agency adoption)
+ Colorado
+ Florida (if adoptive parents are identified)
+ Kansas
+ Mississippi
+ Nebraska
+ New Hampshire
+ New Jersey
+ New Mexico
+ Oklahoma
+ Oregon
+ South Carolina
+ Utah
+ West Virginia
+ Wisconsin
+ Wyoming

No revocation at all (unless in the child's best interest):

+ Hawaii
+ Indiana
+ Louisiana (birth fathers only)
+ Massachusetts
+ Nevada
+ New York (private adoption)

+ North Dakota
+ Ohio
+ Rhode Island

Three days:

+ Florida (if adoptive parents not identified)
+ Illinois
+ Maine
+ North Carolina (unborn infants and infants under 3 months of age)

Four days:

+ Iowa

Five days (after birth):

+ Louisiana

Seven days:

+ North Carolina

Ten days:

+ Alaska
+ Arkansas
+ District of Columbia
+ Georgia
+ Minnesota
+ Tennessee

Eleven days:

+ Tennessee

Fourteen days:

+ Alabama

Fifteen days:
- Oklahoma (out of court consents only)
- Virginia

Twenty days:
- Kentucky

Twenty-one days:
- Vermont

Thirty days:
- California (direct placement)
- Maryland

Forty-five days:
- New York (consent made outside of court)

Sixty days:
- Delaware

Any time before final decree:
- Connecticut
- Idaho
- Michigan
- Missouri
- Montana
- Pennsylvania
- South Dakota (final decree takes two years)
- Washington

ADOPTIVE PARENT CONSENT

It is also important to understand that the adoptive parents must give their consent to the adoption. You can change your mind any time until the adoption is finalized by the court. This is something very few adoptive families consider, but it is important to understand your rights. Just because you say you want to adopt a child, you are not obligated to do so. However, if you change your mind, you cannot get a refund on the expenses you have paid. If you adopt a child and later determine that the situation is not going to work, you cannot just give the child back. You need to have your parental rights terminated by the state and you also probably be required to pay for the expenses of foster care up until termination.

Adoption Court Procedures

The actual court procedure for an adoption is the last big hurdle in the process. As previously discussed, revocation of consent is the only real worry facing prospective adoptive parents at this point.

Your adoption will be handled in your state's family, juvenile, or surrogate's court. Your attorney will file your adoption petition and other paperwork. The court will review all the documents, including the home study and background checks. If the birth parents are required to or choose to give consent in front of the judge, this will happen in the courtroom. If the child is of the age set by the state, he or she will be asked to consent to the adoption. If a birth father could not be located and notice was given, the court will review the notice to make sure it meets the state's requirements. The adoptive parents appear in court to tell the court they agree to the adoption. The adoption is then finalized and the judge signs the final order. This makes it official and legal.

There is no testimony, cross-examination, or other courtroom theatrics. Adoption procedures are quiet and simple. There are legalities that must be taken care of, but by the time you go to court to finalize the adoption, all problems should be behind you. Once you have dealt with the consent issues, your adoption is usually very simple.

Adoption proceedings are happy occasions and judges are usually pleased to be part of them. Judges spend most of their time dealing with cases where people are arguing or are unhappy, so it is a pleasant experience for them to handle a case where the result is a happy ending. Most judges will allow family and friends to join you in the courtroom. The court staff will often congratulate the adoptive parents and "ooh" and "ahh" over the adoptive child. When the adoptive child is old enough to speak and understand what is happening, he or she is often made a part of the proceeding as well and is made to feel as if something very special has happened for him or her. Some judges will even give the child a certificate or a card in further recognition of how special the event is. If you wish to take photographs, be sure to check with the court staff beforehand.

Postplacement

With most agency adoptions, you will have some *postplacement* contact with the agency or with a social worker. You may have one or two postplacement visits from the social worker to make sure things are going smoothly and to offer some assistance with adjustments. These visits are usually nothing to worry about. The worker is not going to rip your child from your arms and take him or her back. The worker will prepare a postplacement report that is filed with the agency and may be filed with the court if required in your state.

Note: *A child may be placed with you before the adoption is finalized. This happens because a birth mother gives birth and knows she wants to place the child, but it takes time for the actual finalization to occur.*

Postplacement visits are not about determining if the adoption should be allowed. They are about making sure you have support and helping the agency see that it went well. Postplacement visits cannot undo an adoption; however, if a worker notices a child is being neglected or abused, it could open up a court procedure to deal with the situation. Once your state has finalized and legalized your adoption, you have nothing to worry about unless a post-placement visit is required before finalization in your state.

Birth Certificates

After the adoption is finalized, you need to get an amended birth certificate for your adopted child. Your attorney will request this form. The new birth certificate will list the adoptive parents, but maintain the child's birth date. This will be your child's official, legal birth certificate. The old birth certificate still exists as a state record, but it is not accessible. The adoption court proceeding also becomes sealed and not accessible. This is why you hear about adult adoptees having difficulty finding their birth parents. The information about the birth becomes inaccessible to protect privacy.

Many states now have their adoption forms online. Check your state court system's website for your state's forms. For example, you can see New York's forms at:
www.courts.state.ny.us/forms/familycourt/adoption.shtml

If you are interested in an adoption where information about the birth parents is accessible to the child, information is available later in this book. (See Chapter 2 for more information about open adoptions.)

Adoption Financial Credits

Once you adopt, under the *Hope for Children Act*, you are entitled to up to a $10,000 deduction (as of the time this book was
published) for the expenses associated with your adoption that
you have not been reimbursed for on your income tax return. If
you adopt a special needs child, you are entitled to the full
deduction (with some income restrictions) without having to
show expenses. Additionally, if you cannot take the full deduction, you can *carry forward* (take in later years) the remaining
amounts. Talk to your accountant or tax preparer about this
credit. (Second-parent adoptions do not qualify.)

Additionally, once your child has been adopted, you can list
him or her as a dependant on your federal taxes, so make sure you
let your tax preparer know about the adoption. Some states also
offer adoption tax credits, so inquire about this. Once you are a
parent, there are other child related tax breaks available, including
deductions for child care. Sit down with your tax preparer and find
out how you can best approach taxes as a new parent.

Many employers offer adoption expense reimbursement (a survey found that 98% of the top 837 U.S. employers provided some
kind of assistance). Check with your human resource manager to
find out if your company offers such a program. Employer assistance is not taxed, so this is yet another tax break.

If your company does not currently offer an adoption
assistance program, information about starting one
is available through:

The Adoption-Friendly Workplace Program

877-777-4222

www.adopt.org/workplace

Family Leave

The federal *Family and Medical Leave Act* allows parents to take unpaid time off from work to care for a newly adopted child (as well as ill family members and for the birth of biological children) within the first twelve months after placement of the child.

NOTE: *The Act will only apply to children that are your own, so taking time off before your adoption is finalized is not covered under the act, unless you have some other reason you can use for taking the time (caring for yourself or another family member).*

You must work for an employer with at least fifty employees and you must have been employed at least twelve months and worked at least 1250 hours. You can take up to twelve total weeks leave in a twelve month period. If you and your spouse work for the same employer, you are only given twelve weeks total between you to split. You can take all the leave at once or spread the leave out so that you work some or all of the time on a part time basis. When possible, you must give thirty days notice of the leave. When you return to work, your employer must reinstate you to your job or to a similar position.

Some states also have family leave laws, so be sure to check with your human resource manager to determine if you are entitled to additional state leave. The states that currently have state family leave acts are:

+ California
+ Connecticut
+ District of Columbia
+ Hawaii
+ Maine
+ Minnesota
+ New Jersey
+ Oregon

+ Rhode Island
+ Vermont
+ Washington
+ Wisconsin

Additionally, California has a state disability law that says that parents of newborns, as well as parents of newly adopted children of any age, qualify for a disability leave that provides the new parents with a percentage of their pay as well as job security. You may also qualify for paid maternity or paternity leave or special adoption leave under your company's policies.

Insurance and Planning for the Future

Once the child is placed with you, you can contact your health insurance company about adding the child to your policy. You will need to have family coverage to add your child. If you do not have family coverage, you may need to wait until the next enrollment period (which usually occurs four times per year) to change your coverage to family coverage. If you have family coverage already, contact your insurer before the adoption is finalized and ask what you need to do to have the child added. You want to be sure your child is covered from the moment of the adoption forward, so this means starting the paperwork before the adoption is completed.

Life Insurance

If you do not already have life insurance, it is a good idea to consider purchasing some. If you are married, you will probably want to name your spouse as beneficiary. If you are unmarried, you will want to name your child as beneficiary. Some parents also like to purchase life insurance for their new child, but it is often a better idea to create an investment account for the child.

You may also wish to consider creating a 529 college savings account for your child to help defray the expenses of a college education. There are many options and it is important to create a complete financial plan for your family. Talk to your financial planner.

WILLS

You will also want to have a will drawn up. Once you adopt a child, he or she inherits from you through the laws of your state, so a will is not important for that reason. It is important because in your will you can name a *guardian* who would have custody of your child should you die (and if your spouse or partner should also die). When choosing a guardian, be sure to choose someone who has similar beliefs as yours and who will be close to your child. Be sure to talk this decision over with the potential guardian. If the guardian you name is unable or unwilling to take on the responsibility of guardianship, the court will find a replacement among your family members, but you want to have a hand in this decision. Name an alternate guardian in case something happens to your first choice.

Read your state's adoption laws at:
www.law.cornell.edu/topics/Table_Adoption.htm

Chapter 4

Second-Parent Adoption

Second-parent adoptions are often referred to as *stepparent adoptions*. The child lives with one legal parent and the child's other parent may be deceased, completely out of touch, or without custody. This legal parent remarries and the stepparent wishes to adopt the child. These adoptions are quite common and are generally simpler than other kinds of adoptions.

If a stepparent does not adopt the child, he or she might have an important parental role in the child's life, but in the eyes of the law, he or she has no authority over or legal connection to the child. The child cannot inherit from the stepparent (unless the stepparent leaves something to him or her in a will) or receive any survivor benefits from the stepparent. The stepparent cannot make medical decisions or educational decisions for the child (unless specifically authorized by the parent) and if the stepparent and the legal parent divorce or break up, the stepparent has no legal right to spend time with the child or seek custody or visitation. Additionally, if the legal parent dies, the stepparent would not automatically be named as the child's guardian or be given custody.

Stepparents often assume a parental role in the child's life, but are lacking any kind of legal role. A stepparent or second-parent adoption legalizes the role the stepparent already has in the child's life.

Deciding to Adopt a Stepchild

The decision to adopt a stepchild should not be made lightly. Once you adopt your stepchild, he or she is your child and the adoption cannot be undone (although in some states there is a short window in which consent to the adoption can be withdrawn). You will be financially and legally responsible for the child and should you get divorced, you could be liable for child support. A stepchild who is adopted becomes your legal child in all ways.

A stepchild that you adopt is able to inherit from you. If you have other children, this adopted stepchild will be treated exactly the same as your other children when it comes to inheritance. Sometimes this can cause bad feelings in families. If you want your adopted stepchild to be treated differently, it is important that you have a will made specifying what you want to leave to each child.

If the child's other parent is deceased, the adoption might be an emotional issue for the child. Some children are resistant to the idea of a stepparent replacing the deceased parent and want to reserve a special role for that parent. In this kind of situation, it is a good idea to explore the child's feelings and possibly seek some family counseling to help sort it out. It may take some time for the child to be ready to take this step. Some stepparents never adopt their stepchildren and there is nothing wrong with that choice either.

Another stumbling block in second-parent adoptions is the way the legal parent and the stepparent feel. Some stepparents are hesitant to take on a legal role in the child's life. Particularly if they do not have biological children of their own, some stepparents feel unsure about the responsibilities of parenthood. It can also be daunting to feel as if you are taking over for a parent who is deceased or out of the picture.

In other situations, the marriage might be experiencing some trouble and the parent and stepparent might see the adoption as providing some additional glue to help hold it together. It is important to understand that a stepparent adoption is not a quick fix for marital problems.

A newly married couple might feel as if they need to hurry to do a stepparent adoption in order to make their new family complete. However, it may simply be too soon in the relationship for the adoption to feel right for the child and everyone else involved.

If you have other children and you are adopting your stepchild, you need to consider the feelings of your children. Some children feel that the adopted child will somehow usurp their positions. It is similar to the way a child feels when a sibling is born into the family, but is more intense because your children clearly know that this new child is not related to you or the rest of the family in quite the same way. Taking some time to help your existing children accept the adoption will help everyone adjust. It is a good idea to have open and frank discussions with everyone in the family about the adoption. Family counseling can help you work through many problems.

If you adopt a stepchild, your parents become your adopted child's grandparents. This can go smoothly or cause some problems. If you have been married to the child's parent for a long time, the child has probably already established a relationship with your parents. If this is a relatively new situation, it may take some time. Regardless of how things have been up to this point, it is important that your parents understand that this child is now fully and completely yours, and by extension, theirs. They should work hard to make sure they treat all of their grandchildren equally or there is sure to be resentment.

It is important that second-parent adoptions are done for the right reason—to solidify a relationship that has already been established between the stepparent and the child and to provide legal rights to the child and stepparent.

Qualifications to Adopt

If you are married to the child's legal parent, you can seek a second-parent adoption. In some states you do not have to be married, but can simply be partners. (See Chapter 11 for information about same-sex couples.) It is usually best to wait until you have been married at least one year before seeking to adopt your stepchild. This demonstrates to the court that you have had time to establish a close relationship with the child and that your marriage is stable (some states require this).

Notice or Consent

The parent that has custody of the child must consent to the adoption and in some states must actually readopt the child as well (so that you are adopting the child together as a couple). While this seems silly, it is simply a formality and does nothing to change the relationship between the child and the existing parent.

If your stepchild has another legal or biological parent that is alive, then that parent is entitled to some kind of notice of the adoption and the chance to deny consent. This other parent must consent to give up all rights to the child or fail to respond to the legal notice that is given in order for the adoption to occur. This legal notice is done by giving the parent papers explaining the intention to adopt the child. In some states these documents can be mailed to the parent or personally *served* (given to him or her in person by a process server). If the other parent cannot be located, you may need to go through a process in which the notice is published in a newspaper.

Stepparent adoption is also possible when the parent has had his or her parental rights terminated by the court (such as in an abuse or neglect situation). In some states, if the other parent does not give consent, his or her rights can be terminated in certain circumstances, for example, if he or she has not had any contact with the child for a long period of time.

If you give the biological parent notice and he or she does not consent, the only way to get around it is to prove neglect and have his or her parental rights terminated or to show the parent has abandoned the child. There is no way to force a biological parent to agree to an adoption, even if the adoption would clearly be in the best interest of the child. If you are in a situation where the biological parent will not consent and you cannot find a way to terminate rights, remember that being a parent is really a state of mind. You can think of yourself as the child's parent and act like his or her parent even if the law will not recognize you as such. Some families that have confronted this problem act as if the step-parent is really a parent. Once the child is an adult, you can legally adopt him or her then to make it official. What makes a parent is what one does, not what a piece of paper says.

Preadoption Procedures

Some states waive the requirement of a home study in second-parent adoptions; some states have laws that require it, but permit judges to waive it; and, other states require stepparents (and the child's existing parent if he or she must also adopt the child) to go through the home study and background check process. Usually when a home study is required, the primary focus will be on the stepparent, his or her history, how long they have been married, and what kind of relationship he or she has with the child. However, when it is required, the home study process is usually minimal. The state department of social services usually performs the home study when it is required.

The states that do not require home studies for second-parent adoptions include:

+ Alabama
+ Alaska

- ✦ Arizona
- ✦ California
- ✦ Colorado
- ✦ Connecticut
- ✦ Florida
- ✦ Georgia
- ✦ Maryland
- ✦ Michigan
- ✦ Minnesota
- ✦ Mississippi
- ✦ Nebraska
- ✦ Ohio
- ✦ Pennsylvania
- ✦ South Carolina
- ✦ Texas

The areas where home studies can be waived for second-parent adoptions include:

- ✦ Arizona
- ✦ District of Columbia
- ✦ Missouri
- ✦ Nevada
- ✦ New Hampshire
- ✦ Oklahoma
- ✦ Oregon
- ✦ Utah

Second-Parent Adoption Process

Stepparent adoptions can be handled on your own without an attorney more easily than other types of adoption, although it is a good idea to hire an attorney to ensure that the case is handled properly. Some states require representation by an attorney.

If you do choose to handle the adoption on your own, you need to contact the court in your state that does adoptions to obtain forms and get information about the filing procedures.

A second-parent adoption follows the same procedure as any other adoption, with the only difference being the home study is sometimes not required. (See Chapter 3 for more details on adoption procedures.)

In many states when a second parent adopts the child, the biological parent that he or she is married to must also adopt the child, so that both people must complete the paperwork. This does nothing to change the biological parent's status and is simply an antiquated procedure. It used to be that only married couples could adopt a child. Some states still require that the second-parent adoption be done by both parents so that both names go through the entire process and both names end up on the birth certificate at the end of the process.

Chapter 5

Kinship Adoption

Kinship adoption occurs when the birth parents are unable to care for a child (or are no longer in the child's life) and some member of the child's family seeks to adopt him or her. Kinship adoptions are considered to be an important way to provide children with continuity of family and culture. They are also less stressful for the child and birth parents. Many times when a parent becomes unable to care for a child, the grandparents or other relatives step in and become caregivers for the child. However, these family caregivers need to have legal authority to make decisions for the child in order to be effective caregivers. Kinship adoptions also allow children to have continuing contact with their birth parent(s) or to at least have access to information about them.

Types of Kinship Adoptions

The most common kinship adoption is adoption by the child's grandparents. This often happens when the birth parents are young or unable to care for the child. Kinship adoption also commonly includes adoption by aunts or uncles.

When talking about kinship adoption it is important to understand that there are two kinds. There are kinship adoptions that are given *special treatment* by states, which simplifies the process. Then there are kinship adoptions that are treated as *regular adop-*

tions, but in which the child happens to be related to the adoptive parents in some way. While this second kind of adoption can be wonderful for helping a child maintain ties and identity, it has no special legal status. (This chapter discusses kinship adoptions that are given special recognition by the states.)

The *AARP Grandparent Information Center* is an excellent resource for grandparents who are raising or planning on adopting their grandchildren. Find information on it at:
www.aarp.org/confacts/programs/gic.html

Adoption versus Guardianship

When a grandparent or other relative assumes the care for a child, a fast way to obtain authority and legality is through a *guardianship* process. Guardianship is a legal decision by a court that one person should have legal and financial decision making power over another person, such as a child or person who is mentally incompetent. Guardianship proceedings maintain the court as having final authority over the child and the court can, at any time, end the guardianship that has been given to the relative. Children cared for by a guardian do not usually qualify for the guardian's health-care plan and cannot inherit from their guardians (unless specified in a will), but adoptive children can.

NOTE: *Guardianship normally only happens with the consent of the parent or if the child has been placed into foster care and the state social services department consents to the guardianship.*

Because guardianship is not permanent, many relatives prefer to seek an adoption as a final resolution for the child. Adoption offers the child permanency and creates a parent-child bond in a way that guardianship cannot.

Custody versus Adoption

Because a parent's right to his or her child is considered to be important, it is almost never possible for a relative, even a grandparent, to take a parent to court and seek custody or the right to adopt the child. Grandparents' rights are considered secondary to parental rights and only in the most extreme cases will a grandparent be given custody of a child against a parent's wishes.

Adoption versus Foster Care

Some kinship adoptions are done from kinship foster care arrangements. Kinship foster care is a wonderful alternative to traditional foster care, but again it fails to offer permanency to the child. While foster care children receive state subsidies, adoptive children do not receive subsidies or do not receive the same amount of subsidy, making this a disadvantage to adopting your kinship foster care child. Foster care also involves supervision by the state, whereas adoption is not supervised once it is finalized.

Notice and Consent

Notice and consent laws apply to kinship adoptions, just as they do to stepparent adoptions. (See Chapter 4 for more information.) However, in most instances the birth parents provide consent and often suggest the adoption. The same revocation rules apply as for all adoptions. If the child is of the age specified by the state, he or she must provide consent as well.

Kinship Agreements

Because kinship adoptions serve to continue a child's bonds with family members and cultural identity, some birth parents create *kinship agreements* with the adoptive parents. Also known as *postadoption contracts* or *cooperative adoption agreements*, these agreements continue the child's relationship with the birth parents.

Sometimes these agreements are informal understandings within the family. While the legal relationship between the child and birth parents has ended and the adoptive parents become the legal parents, the family has an understanding that the child will know who his or her mother or father is and may even continue to refer to him or her that way.

Some states formally recognize kinship agreements and make them part of the adoption decree. The court can enforce the agreements and makes sure the parties comply with them. However, failure to comply with the agreement usually cannot provide the basis for revoking or invalidating the adoption. The agreements are important because they provide a lasting link to the biological family. There is no compliance mechanism because the only solution would be to undo the adoption. That is not a solution that will help the children in the long run.

Kinship agreements are forward thinking arrangements meant to better a child's life. Sometimes they do not work out, but it is usually in the child's best interest to try to follow them. Often if a child is over the age of twelve, he or she must consent to the kinship agreement.

States that enforce kinship agreements include:
+ California
+ Florida
+ Indiana
+ Minnesota
+ Nebraska
+ Nevada
+ New Mexico
+ Oregon
+ Rhode Island
+ Washington

Some birth parents fail to understand the level of access granted to them by kinship agreements. These agreements never give a birth parent the right to change his or her mind about the adoption, permanently take the child, or make decisions for the child. The agreements simply provide a framework for giving the child a lasting connection with the birth parents or other relatives.

Kinship agreements can also be important if siblings are adopted into different homes or families. It is often difficult to find adoptive parents that can accept sibling groups. If the children are to be adopted, it is often done separately. The court can issue a kinship order, requiring that the siblings continue to see each other and be part of each other's lives.

Agency Involvement

Kinship adoptions can be done privately (without an agency) or with an agency. Often the agency involved is the local public agency. If the agency places a foster child with a relative, the agency will continue to be involved throughout the process of freeing the child for adoption or obtaining consent from the birth parents. (See Chapter 6 for more information about agency adoptions.)

Court Proceedings

The court process for kinship adoptions is no different than those for other adoptions, except that there may not be an agency involved. (See Chapter 3 for more information about court proceedings.) Some states require home studies, while others do not. Additionally, judges are sometimes permitted to waive the requirement. If a home study is required, it is done by the state department of social services and is normally brief. The states that do not require home studies for kinship adoptions include:

- ✦ Alabama
- ✦ Alaska
- ✦ Arizona

- ✦ California
- ✦ Colorado
- ✦ Florida
- ✦ Georgia
- ✦ Illinois
- ✦ Maine
- ✦ Maryland
- ✦ Michigan
- ✦ Mississippi
- ✦ Missouri
- ✦ Montana
- ✦ New Mexico
- ✦ North Carolina
- ✦ Ohio
- ✦ Pennsylvania
- ✦ Rhode Island
- ✦ South Carolina
- ✦ Texas
- ✦ Washington
- ✦ West Virginia

The areas where home studies can be waived include:
- ✦ District of Columbia
- ✦ Iowa
- ✦ Kansas
- ✦ Nevada
- ✦ New Hampshire
- ✦ Oklahoma
- ✦ Oregon
- ✦ Utah
- ✦ Vermont

Finalization

Once a kinship adoption is complete, the new birth certificate will be issued listing the adoptive parents, even if there is a kinship agreement in place allowing the child contact with the birth parents. (See Chapter 3 for information about birth certificates.)

Kinship adoptions provide children with stability and security while maintaining a full sense of family history and connections.

> *Generations United* is an organization that provides information and support to kinship caregivers. Their website contains information about financial assistance, respite care, support, and housing. It also has detailed information on specific state laws about kinship care and adoption. Contact them at:
>
> *Generations United*
> 1333 H. Street, NW
> Suite 500 W
> Washington, DC 20005
> 202-289-3979
> **www.gu.org**

Support

Raising a child you have adopted through a kinship adoption has benefits and drawbacks. A huge benefit is that the child was already part of your family and was probably familiar to you before you adopted. This makes the adjustment process simpler for everyone.

However, often children adopted through kinship adoptions can be confused about the change in their family—it is still familiar but not the same. Additionally, while it is wonderful that your child may continue to know and have contact with his or her birth parents, as well as the rest of the birth family, there is potential for conflict with birth parents who think they should still have a say in the child's life or birth relatives who do not understand their new roles.

It takes time to allow the entire family to adjust to a kinship adoption and for everyone to accept their new roles. Kinship agreements can be helpful for laying out roles and boundaries, but as an adoptive parent you must make certain everyone understands that you are your child's parent and as such you will be making all decisions for him or her from now on.

If you are a grandparent who has adopted your grandchild, you can find help and support through websites such as:

www.grandsplace.com

and

www.grandparentagain.com

Chapter 6

Domestic Agency Adoption

Most people who adopt use an agency to help them locate a birth mother or a child, and to help process the adoption. If you are adopting a child born in the United States, the agency you use will be a *domestic agency*. Domestic agencies are not all alike. The first important distinction is between public and private agencies. A *public agency* refers to a state department of social services or department of family and children's services. These agencies handle the adoption of children who were in foster care and have been freed for adoption by the state's courts or who have been surrendered by their birth parents. Most of these children are not babies and many are special needs children. There are many children available for adoption through these state agencies.

Private agencies are those run by private entities. Some are non-profit, while others are for-profit businesses. Some are run by religious organizations, while others are nonsectarian. You will find that there is a wide selection of private agencies to choose from.

Public Agencies

Public agency adoptions have the same requirements as other types of adoptions, including the home study, background check, and court procedure to finalize the adoption. Public agency adoptions are usually the fastest and least expensive type of adoption. However, since the children tend to be older, the transition and adjustment period is often more difficult.

All children that are available for adoption in a state are shown in the state's photolisting book. (See Appendix B for links to state photolisting books.) The books show a photo and description of each child.

There are several ways to adopt a child through a public agency.

FOSTER CARE

The *foster care* system is set up to provide a home for children who have been removed from their homes because of abuse, neglect, and occasionally due to juvenile delinquency. Children who have been abandoned or voluntarily placed with the state by parents are also placed in foster care. These children are placed in the temporary care of the state while their parents deal with the court system or the court determines that their parents abandoned them. Many times these children are returned to their parents if the court decides that no abuse or neglect occurred or if the parents meet the requirements set up by the agency (such as counseling, child care classes, maintaining a stable lifestyle, and so on) and the parents are deemed fit to care for the children.

In other instances, the children never return home. Most states now make an effort to move the case through the court system quickly so that the children are either returned home or are freed for adoption and do not languish in foster care for years. The federal *Adoption and Safe Families Act* states that if a child has been in foster care for at least fifteen months or if his or her parents abandoned the child, the parental rights can be terminated and the child can be freed for adoption. For the children that do not return home, the court severs the biological parents' ties to the children and frees them for adoption.

Many adoptions occur by the foster parents who care for the children while their case is pending or while their parents are trying to meet the agency's requirements for return. Becoming a foster parent is one route to public agency adoption. To become a foster parent, you must first identify the private agencies that contract for foster care with the state. In most states, the public agency itself does not directly handle foster care placement. Prospective foster care parents must work with a public agency that handles the state agency's contract for foster care.

> Find contacts for foster care agencies in your state at:
> **http://fosterparenting.adoption.com/agencies/agencies.php**
>
> Get support and information about foster care adoption at:
> **www.DaveThomasFoundationforAdoption.org**

To become a foster parent you must:

+ complete a series of classes;
+ provide financial, personal, and health information about yourself and your family;
+ be able to provide appropriate housing for a child or children;
+ be prepared for ongoing contact with caseworkers; and,
+ understand that a foster care parent's job is to care for the child, while helping to reunite him or her with the biological parents. (Adoption is not an option until the child has been freed for adoption.)

When you become a foster parent, you will make yourself available to children who may or may not be freed for adoption. At the time of initial placement, you have no way of knowing how the case will ultimately be resolved. As a foster parent, you will receive a small monthly stipend that is meant to cover the child's expenses and you will also have to follow the caseworker's instructions. While you are the foster care parent, the child is in the custody of the state and the caseworker will have absolute authority over major decisions involving the child. Foster parents have very little rights when it comes to the children they care for.

Contact your local public agency for information about which private agencies handle foster care and how you can apply.

LEGAL RISK PLACEMENT

Legal risk placement occurs when you accept a child that you would like to adopt who has not yet been completely freed for adoption. The intent of the placement is for the child to begin to develop a relationship with you and to begin to put down roots. However, the child is not legally free for adoption yet and something may happen that could prevent the adoption from happening. While you are waiting for the child to be freed for adoption, you are acting as a foster care parent since the state has custody and control of the child. This kind of placement allows you to get a jump on the whole process by bonding with your child before the finalization, but you must accept the risk that the adoption may not be finalized.

TRADITIONAL ADOPTION

Another method of adopting a child through a public agency is the traditional method, where the child is not placed until the adoption is complete. The child remains in foster care until the legal process is finalized and then comes home to the adoptive parents. This is the least risky of all the public agency adoption choices, but it can also be the most emotionally difficult for a child old enough to understand what is happening. There is no transition period as there is in foster care placement or legal risk placement.

Find your state public adoption agency online at:
www.calib.com/naic/pubs/r_agency.cfm

PUBLIC AGENCY ADOPTION ISSUES

When adopting a child through a public agency, make sure to obtain full medical records and family histories if available. Before you agree to the adoption, you want to get as much information as you can. The child may have a history or background that does not work for you. (It is important to be honest and face the fact that not every child is the right child for you.) The caseworkers who manage the child while he or she is in foster care have access to the biological parents and can obtain this information. They can also provide information about assessments and evaluations that have been done while the child has been in foster care.

Because the child is usually leaving parents that are alive and have some kind of relationship with the child (no matter how dysfunctional), there are significant transition issues for the child and the adoptive parent. If the child is old enough, he or she will remember his or her biological parents and will have some kind of attachment to them, even if they were terrible parents. It takes a lot of time and patience to help children adjust. It also takes time for them to learn to trust adoptive parents. Many of these children were abused, malnourished, or emotionally damaged.

Moving into a loving, nurturing home can be a shock. Some adoptive parents report that their new children would raid the refrigerator and gorge—certain that soon they would starve again. Other children have been known to steal from new family members or harm new siblings. There are numerous behavioral issues you might face after the adoption. A good counselor or therapist is essential to help everyone make a smooth adjustment. Your social worker from the agency can provide some help with adjustment or can recommend a private counselor. It is also a good idea to get involved with an adoption support group.

Get tips on helping an older child deal with adoption at:
www.familyhelper.net/arc/old.html

SPECIAL NEEDS

Many public agency adoptive children have special needs. Special needs children are those that take longer to place and include:

+ school age children or teens;
+ children with physical, mental, or emotional disabilities;
+ sibling groups that must stay together; and,
+ children of certain racial or ethnic groups that are difficult to place.

Simply because a child is described as special needs does not mean that there is anything wrong with him or her. It just means that this child is one that is difficult to place. Your home might be the perfect place for a special needs child. For this reason it is important to find out what evaluations have been done, what the specialists recommend, and what kind of care or treatment the child needs.

Learn about the child's exposure to or use of drugs or alcohol and have a treatment plan in place to deal with these issues. Get detailed information about the child's behavior and where he or she has lived and who has cared for him or her in the past. Ask for copies of all reports, evaluations, and assessments.

The *National Resource Center for Special Needs Adoption* can provide information and support for those adopting special needs children. Contact them at:
National Resource Center for Special Needs Adoption
16250 Northland Dr. Suite 120
Southfield, MI 48075
248-443-0306
www.nrcadoption.org/index.htm
Other sites that can provide information include:
www.special-needs.adoption.com and
www.spaulding.org

Special needs children may appeal to people who do not wish to care for a baby or toddler, or who have special skills dealing with disabled children or in working with teens. Additionally, special needs children are sometimes easier to adopt because the agency is willing to overlook certain problems with the adoptive family in order to help the children find a home.

Adopting a special needs child can be a challenge, but it can also be tremendously rewarding. Special needs kids often recognize the fact that they are hard to place. Sometimes the adjustment process can be difficult because they tend to erect barriers since they have had their hopes dashed so many times in the past. Adopting a special needs child does not work for everyone, but many families find it to be rewarding.

FINANCIAL ASSISTANCE FOR PUBLIC AGENCY ADOPTIONS

Because of the difficult nature of many public agency adoptions and because many of the children adopted do have special needs, there is special funding available to assist the parents in caring for the child after the adoption.

Title IV-E Assistance

Special needs children may qualify for federal funding assistance. The child may be receiving Social Security Insurance (SSI) payments already, but may also qualify for *Adoption and Safe Families Act* (ASFA) funding. ASFA provides financial assistance for children who are adopted and:

+ were receiving Temporary Assistance to Needy Families (TANF) in other words, welfare, in the birth home or

+ were eligible for SSI in the birth home which means they were disabled and were in a home that met certain financial requirements.

When you are negotiating your adoption with your public agency, you need to ask about eligibility for this funding. You can apply directly through your local social services or family services department. Usually the social worker who handles your adoption will help you apply.

For more information about state subsidies, visit:
www.adopting.org/subsidy.html

Adoption Assistance Agreement

An *adoption assistance agreement* is a contract between the adoptive parents and the state agency, describing the ongoing monthly payments the state will make to the parents after the adoption is complete to help with the expense of raising the child. The payments are often for a few hundred dollars per month.

The agreement is made before the adoption takes place and is in effect as long as the child is a minor. The agreement may also include provisions for assistance with the child's medical expenses (see the Medicaid section later in this chapter). Some states include additional funding amounts for children that are especially difficult to care for. These are known as Level of Care (LOC) payments.

These agreements are common for special needs adoptions where the child is known to need continuing care or services that are outside of the normal medical needs children experience. They are provided so that families will adopt these children and not have to worry about affording the care the child will need.

> For information on what your state pays for adoption assistance, see:
> **www.nacac.org/subsidy_stateprofiles.html**

The agreement is enforceable. If there is future disagreement about it, an administrative hearing is held to resolve the problem. Do not finalize your adoption until this document is signed.

If you negotiate an agreement, make sure it:

+ is in writing;
+ contains beginning and ending dates for the payments;
+ specifies the amount of payments and any changes to the amount as the child ages;
+ does not put excessive restrictions or requirements on you after the adoption occurs;
+ specifies the reporting or certification you need to comply with to continue to receive payments;
+ lists all services to be provided by the state;
+ explains how subsidies or services can be increased or decreased and what kind of notice is required;
+ describes Medicaid coverage for the child;
+ explains what happens if you move out of state or if both adoptive parents die;
+ describes what you need to do to get an administrative hearing should you need one; and,
+ takes into account your child's needs and your family's situation.

Medicaid

A special needs child may qualify for *Medicaid*. The state Medicaid program will pay many of his or her medical expenses both before and after the adoption. If you have a family health care policy, your child can also receive treatment under that plan—it may cover some of the things that Medicaid does not. Medicaid is a federal program, but is administered by each state individually with different rights and procedures in each state. Your social worker will provide information about your child's Medicaid eligibility.

For more information about Medicaid, visit:
www.cms.hhs.gov/medicaid

Tax Credits

Parents adopting a special needs child are entitled to a $10,000 tax credit, without having to show any expenses. This applies to families earning under $150,000 per year. Those earning between $150,000 and $189,999 receive a reduced credit in proportion to income. This is a credit that is nonrefundable—meaning that you cannot get money refunded above your tax liability. But if you do have a lower income, you can claim the credit over a five year period so that you can use more of it. There are also some state tax credits available, also you should check with your tax preparer to find out what your state provides. (See Chapter 3 for more information about tax credits.)

For the purposes of the tax credit, a special needs child is one who cannot be placed with adoptive parents without providing a subsidy. A reasonable, but unsuccessful effort must be made to place the child for adoption without a subsidy, unless it is in the child's best interests to remain with prospective adoptive parents with whom they have significant emotional ties. Factors or conditions related to the special needs determination may include ethnic background, age, membership in a minority or sibling group, the presence of a medical condition, or physical, mental, or emotional disabilities.

IRS Publication 968 explains tax credits in more details. Find it at:

www.irs.gov

Other Assistance

Organizations for parents of special needs children (including those referenced earlier in this chapter) will provide support and assistance as you adopt and raise a special needs child. If your child is of school age, or will soon be of school age, you will need to begin to learn your way around the special education process.

For information and resources about special education, visit:
www.seriweb.com

The federal *Department of Education* has a section about special education located at:
www.ed.gov/about/offices/list/osers/osep/index.html

Wrights Law is an excellent site devoted to helping parents navigate the system. Find it at:
www.wrightslaw.com

The *National Dissemination Center for Children with Disabilities* is another excellent resource. Find it at:
www.nichcy.org

Some states provide special tuition assistance or waivers for foster care children who have been adopted. For information, see:
www.nacac.org/subsidyfactsheets/tuition.html

Biological Relatives

Another important issue is the child's *biological relatives*. While a court can sever legal ties between a child and his or her biological family, the court cannot change the emotional ties that exist when an older child is adopted. For this reason, some courts permit adoptive parents and biological relatives of the child to create and record kinship agreements. These agreements set out a plan for how the child will continue to have contact with important family members (such as grandparents, siblings, aunts and uncles). This prevents a child from feeling totally cut off from his or her family and ethnic heritage. (See Chapter 5 for more information about kinship agreements.)

Agency Liability

All agencies have a duty to fully disclose information about the child being placed for adoption. This duty is particularly important when working with a public agency, since most children placed through it have had difficult home lives or suffer disabilities. The agency must disclose to you:

+ how and why the child came into the state's care;
+ why the child remained in the care of the state;
+ why the parental rights were terminated; and,
+ why the agency decided to place the child.

It is also important that the case worker explain to you the causal relationship that exists between a child's home life and his or her behavior—how the things he or she went through have caused him or her to act the way he or she does and how it might impact future behavior. The caseworker is responsible for reading the entire file and disclosing all the information in it to you. Failure to do so is negligence on the part of the agency.

There is some dispute about how far a worker must go. Some states say that a caseworker should make reasonable efforts to investigate the background of the family the child came from, while most states say that the agency is not required to take investigative steps.

The child's file should include the following:

+ hospital records;
+ records from doctor's offices;
+ the child's HIV history (including testing);
+ school records; and,
+ what family background is known.

An agency that fails to disclose all of this information can be sued for *wrongful adoption*. Some agencies in the past have placed a child and lied about his or her history or purposefully failed to disclose important information. When a court finds that wrongful adoption has occurred, money damages are awarded. These damages can be *punitive* (to punish the agency) and can also be *compensatory*, to pay back the family for the medical or psychological care it has had to pay that it did not anticipate. Sometimes damages are also awarded to pay the family back for physical harm caused by the adoptive child (if, for example, the child has caused damage to property or harmed family members). The family cannot recover the ordinary costs of raising a child. In a few rare cases, the family has been allowed to dissolve the adoption and return the child to the agency.

The best way to avoid these kinds of problems is to insist on complete disclosure, to go over documents carefully, and to use an adoption attorney who will help you make sure your rights are protected.

The *Child Welfare League of America* publishes standards that public adoption agencies should try to follow. Find more information at:

www.cwla.org

Private Agency Adoption

Private agencies have infants as well as older children to place for adoption. An infant will take the longest to adopt (because you may need to wait for one to be born), while older children are placed more quickly. Most parents using private agencies are looking for babies.

EVALUATING A PRIVATE AGENCY

The first step to working with a private agency is to carefully select one. Since you will pay an application fee, it is usually not a good idea to apply to more than one agency at a time. Be sure to evaluate agencies carefully. (See Chapter 6 for more information about this.)

To find a list of private agencies in your area to search for licensed adoption agencies in your state, visit the *National Adoption Information Clearinghouse* website at: **www.calib.com/naic/database/nadd/naddsearch.cfm**

Once you have narrowed down your search to a few agencies, talk to the adoption specialist at your state department of social services. (See Appendix B for information.) He or she can tell you what the agencies are like and what kind of information the state has available about them. Check with the Better Business Bureau in your state to determine if any complaints have been filed against the agency. Talk with other adoptive parents and find out what they have heard about the agency.

FEES

Compare the home study costs and other fees that each agency charges. Less might not always be better if you feel a more expensive agency does a better job. Be absolutely certain that the agency and the social worker who does the home study are licensed in your state. Most states do not set limits on the fees an agency may charge, but do require that they must not exceed what is considered *reasonable and customary*. Cost can range anywhere from $4,000 to $30,000, depending on the agency. Agencies run by religious groups tend to cost less. Some agencies charge a flat fee, while others charge for each service separately. Be sure to get a complete list of what is covered by a flat fee.

The following are fees typically charged and the average cost of each. Your costs may be higher or lower but this list gives a rough estimate of what to expect to pay in fees. The average costs include:

+ application—$250;
+ home study—$1200;
+ post placement services—$500;
+ psychological evaluations of parents—$200 each;
+ physical exams for parents—$75 each;
+ document fees—varies (often $1000);
+ court fees and legal costs varies by state—up to $12,000;
+ advertising fees—$2000;
+ birth mother living costs—varies;
+ medical expenses for mother and baby—varies;
+ legal fees for birth mother may be $1000; and,
+ counseling—$1000.

Be sure to compare fees between several agencies so that you have an understanding of what the average fees are like in your area.

You may be asked to pay for most expenses up front or you may be able to pay for them as they occur. Find out how the agency requires you to pay before applying.

EXPENSES

Be skeptical if the agency takes money paid for your birth mother's expenses and places it in an escrow pool out of which it pays all birth mothers' individual expenses for placing babies with the agency. With this method, you do not pay your birth mother's actual expenses, but instead pay an average cost that takes into account high expenses some birth mothers have. Most states require an accounting be made to the court, listing the expenses the adoptive parents have paid for.

Because most of the babies available for placement have not been born yet, there is the very real chance that the birth mother will change her mind before placement occurs. Always find out what the agency's policy is about the fees you have already paid—can you roll them over to use for another birth mother should the birth mother you choose change her mind? Idaho is the only state that requires birth parents to reimburse adoptive parents if the birth parents change their minds and decide not to place the child for adoption.

Some states permit adoptive parents to pay for the birth mother's living expenses during her pregnancy. Adoptive parents pay for the medical expenses of both birth mother and baby. The baby will not be covered by your health insurance plan until the child is placed with you, so these expenses are out of pocket expenses for adoptive parents, unless the birth mother has health insurance coverage (or the adoptive parents purchase a policy for her).

Many adoptive parents feel a need to give the birth mother a gift after the birth. While this may seem like a wonderful gesture, it in fact can cause problems for you since many states prohibit any compensation to the birth mother for the adoption. This is intended to prevent the buying and selling of babies, but also prevents extravagant gifts. Small tokens of appreciation may be acceptable, but you need to check with your agency and your attorney before doing anything. (See Chapter 3 for more information about the length of time living expenses can be paid.)

The following states specifically list certain expenses adoptive parents cannot pay or cap the payments:

+ Connecticut ($1500 limit);
+ Delaware (nothing other than court and legal expenses);
+ Idaho ($2000 limit);

+ Illinois (does not allow lost wages, gifts, and educational expenses);

+ Indiana ($3000 limit);

+ Iowa (nothing other than room and board and counseling);

+ Kentucky (does not allow for payment of birth parents' attorney fees);

+ Maine (nothing other than legal costs, counseling, transportation to services, foster care, and living expenses);

+ Minnesota (does not allow for lost wages, gifts, or educational expenses);

+ Montana (does not allow for education, vehicle, salary, wages, vacations, or permanent housing for birth mother);

+ New Hampshire (no gifts over $50 or educational expenses);

+ New Mexico (nothing other than living expenses, medical costs, travel expenses, counseling and legal/court fees);

+ Ohio (nothing other than medical costs and legal expenses);

+ Utah (nothing other than legal fees and expenses, medical care, maternity expenses, and living expenses); and,

+ Wisconsin (does not permit lost wages or living expenses or anything other than counseling, maternity clothes, medical care, legal fees, birthing classes and a $50 gift).

Interstate Issues

Depending on what state you live in, you may find that there are not many children available to adopt from within your state. If this is the case, you may need to adopt a child that is born in another state. To do so, you and the agency must be in compliance with the *Interstate Compact*, a federal law that governs how children are transported between states for adoption purposes. Each state has an Interstate Compact administrator. The administrators in the state you live in and the state you are adopting from must both agree to the adoption. Your adoption agency and attorney will handle this technicality for you.

Ethnic Concerns

You also need to be aware of a federal law called the *Multiethnic Placement Act.* It denies federal funding to adoption agencies that delay or deny placement because of race (in other words, wait to place a child only with parents of the same race as the child). If you are interested in adopting a child with an ethnic background that is different than yours, ask if the agency complies with this statute. If you believe you have been denied a placement due to race, talk to your adoption attorney or contact your state attorney general.

For support in raising a multiethnic family, contact: *Association of Multiethnic Americans* at:
www.ameasite.org/ipride_.html

Chapter 7

International Adoption

International adoption is the adoption of a child from a country outside the U.S. International adoption has become more popular in recent years with publicity about how many waiting children there are in countries around the world. International adoption is an excellent choice if you do not want to wait to find a birth mother or new baby and do not mind adopting a child who is not a newborn. The procedure is not as complicated as some people expect it to be and the costs end up being about the same when you factor in travel expenses. The procedure is similar to those for domestic adoptions but involves extra steps such as dealing with the United States Department of Homeland Security's Citizenship and Immigration Services (USCIS)—once known as the Immigration and Naturalization Service (INS)—and U.S. and overseas courts.

Choosing an Agency

You will always need to work with an agency to do an international adoption, since children are available only through agencies in foreign countries. Some private agencies handle only domestic adoption or only international adoption, while others handle both types. To find an agency, check with your local agencies, talk to members of your adoption support group, or join a group specifically for international adoptive families to find out which agency parents used.

You can search for agencies by the country you wish to adopt from or by the state you live in at:

http://directory.adoption.com

The *Joint Council of International Children's Services* has a list of agencies it accredits that can be found at:

www.jcics.org

The *International Adoption Consortium* also has a similar list that can be found at:

www.iacgroup.org

For more information on choosing an international adoption agency, see:

www.adopting.org/choosagn.html

Choosing a Country

At the time this book was written, international adoptions were mainly available from the following countries:

- ✦ Bolivia
- ✦ Bulgaria
- ✦ Cambodia
- ✦ China
- ✦ Columbia
- ✦ Guatemala
- ✦ Haiti
- ✦ India
- ✦ Mexico
- ✦ Philippines
- ✦ Romania
- ✦ Russia and former Soviet republics
- ✦ South Korea
- ✦ Thailand
- ✦ Vietnam

The *U.S. Department of State* has country-specific information available on its website. The document for each country on the site spells out the requirements and U.S. agencies that handle adoptions for that country. Visit it at:

http://travel.state.gov/adopt.html

Each country has its own requirements. Most countries require that a couple be married for at least three years and have age limits. Russia requires that parents make two trips to the country—one to identify the child and the second to adopt him or her.

Some parents go into the adoption process knowing which country they want to adopt from, while others have no preference and choose a country that seems to fit them best. When choosing a country you will want to consider:

- ✦ your feelings about each country's culture and history;
- ✦ your feelings about the physical attributes common to children from that country;
- ✦ your own background and family history;
- ✦ your feeling about raising children of different ethnicity than yours;
- ✦ the type of medical care birth mothers receive in each country;
- ✦ whether or not you need to travel to that country to adopt;
- ✦ the length of stay required and the number of visits required to adopt in each country;
- ✦ the ease with which paperwork is processed in that country; and,
- ✦ the experiences of other adoptive parents who have adopted from that country.

The selection of a country is a matter of personal choice. There is not room in this book to discuss the differences between the various countries, so it is important that you do some research on your own. Start with the U.S. Department of State website and the websites about adoption in the various countries listed in Appendix A.

Choosing a Child

In some countries, you go to the orphanage and actually select a child that appeals to you, while other countries assign a child to you. If you adopt from South Korea, you will not meet your child until he or she is delivered to you at the airport in the U.S.

Medical concerns are important to consider when selecting a child. Because the standard of health care varies greatly overseas, many children available for placement are developmentally delayed or suffer from a minor or major health problem. Before you choose a child, obtain photos, videotape if possible, as well as whatever medical records can be translated into English. Have them reviewed by a pediatrician who specializes in evaluating children for overseas adoptions. If you will not have access to these documents before you travel overseas, make arrangements before you leave to fax or send these items to the doctor while you are there. This kind of doctor can evaluate the child from the records and make an educated inference about what kinds of problems the child is or may be experiencing. Based on the evaluation you may decide to adopt a different child.

The *American Academy of Pediatrics* provides a list of pediatricians specializing in adoption. View the list at:
**www.aap.org/sections/adoption/adopt-states/
adoption-map.html**

It is imperative that the child you select is legally released for adoption by the country of origin. Only children who are completely released for adoption will be eligible for adoption in the eyes of the U.S. government. You will need your agency's help to obtain this release.

You have the right to turn down the child that is offered to you. Often this happens after the medical reports are examined or after you meet the child. Some parents do not wish to adopt a child with serious medical problems, while others are comfortable doing so. This is a matter of personal choice. It is important that you work with professionals you can trust who can give you good advice about medical history and developmental delays.

> For information about how to evaluate an infant, see:
> **http://adoptingfromrussia.com/MedicalEvaluation.html**

If you decide not to accept the child, you do not return to square one. All of the paperwork you have provided will still be valid, but you will have to wait for another child to be selected for you. The process differs in each country. You may have to return home (if you are visiting the country) or you may be able to have another child assigned to you while you are there. Be sure to ask your agency how this process will work when you begin the process so there are no surprises.

Dealing with Paperwork

Your application for the adoption will be made to your local agency. They will be your primary contact throughout the entire adoption process and will handle most of the contact with the overseas agency. The application and home study process for an international adoption is similar to that required for a domestic adoption, with a few extra steps. All of these documents must be translated and then approved by the agency in the country you are adopting from (your agency will arrange for the translation).

Additionally, many of the documents you provide must be authenticated, meaning they must bear a raised seal from the agency or office issuing them (there is an additional fee for obtaining authenticated copies). You may need to include photos of your home for review by the overseas agency.

In addition to the usual home study and application, you will also need to obtain preliminary USCIS approval. If you are married, one spouse must be a U.S. citizen and your combined income must be 25% above the poverty level. You are not eligible if you have been convicted of a felony or certain misdemeanors.

The Process

Because each country has its own requirements, there is no one set procedure for international adoptions. However, the procedure you must follow in the U.S. is the same.

You will need to complete the application, home study process (your home study will be used both by the agency as well as the USCIS to determine that you are qualified to adopt) and background check (which is also submitted to USCIS). Fingerprints must be completed at a USCIS office using the provided form FD-258. Fingerprinting will occur at your home USCIS office if you are in the U.S. or at an embassy or consulate if you are abroad.

Before you even have a child selected for adoption, you can begin the adoption process by filing form I-600A, **ORPHAN PETITION**. It begins the process of classifying the child you will adopt as an *immediate relative*. The fee for filing is $460. You also need to file form I-864. It is an affidavit about your ability to support a child. All USCIS forms must be filed at your local office. (See Appendix C for a copy of the form.)

You can complete the forms online at:
http://uscis.gov/graphics/formsfee/forms

Once you have been approved to adopt by the agency and the U.S. government, you will need to learn about the requirements for finalizing the adoption in the overseas country your child is from. This may include a court appearance in the country's court. If so, it is important that you have a translator along, which your agency can help you arrange. You may need to travel to the country and stay there for a period of time before you are permitted to adopt. You may need to appear in court in the country to finalize the adoption. Obtain several official copies of any documents you are provided by the officials you work with in the country.

Dealing with Immigration

To bring your child to the U.S., you must do the following.

+ Use form I-600 to petition to have the identified child classified as an *immediate relative*. (If you filed form I-600A there is no fee for form I-600. If you did not, there is a $460 fee).

+ Apply for the child to immigrate to the U.S.

You must physically see your child in person before you are permitted to adopt him or her. If a married couple is adopting, only one member of the couple must see the child in order for the adoption to be valid. If you are not adopting your child abroad and instead are only adopting him or her in the U.S., be sure you check that box on the **ORPHAN PETITION**.

VISAS

A *visa* is a document that gives tentative permission for the child to enter the United States from a foreign country. The visa itself is not complete authority, since immigration officials have the final say upon the child's entrance to the country.

To apply for a visa for your child, use form IR-3, for children adopted in a foreign country, or IR-4, for children that will be adopted in the U.S. The application must be submitted to the U.S. embassy or consular office in the country the child is being adopted from. The child must be seen by the consular or embassy official and must also be examined by a physician approved by the consulate or embassy. Certain contagious diseases may be the basis for temporarily denying a visa. The adoptive parents must appear at the consulate or embassy for an interview. There is a $260 fee to apply for the visa and a $65 fee for the issuance of the visa.

Citizenship

Part of the adoption process is helping your child become a United States citizen. There are several ways this can occur.

CHILD CITIZENSHIP ACT OF 2000

The federal *Child Citizenship Act of 2000* allows an internationally adopted child to automatically become a U.S. citizen. In order for the act to apply, the child must:

+ have one U.S. parent (adoptive);
+ be legally adopted by this parent;
+ be under age 18;
+ live with the U.S. parent that has custody of the child; and,
+ be admitted to the U.S. as an immigrant for lawful permanent residence (under an IR-4 Visa).

If these requirements are satisfied, your child will automatically be granted citizenship when the adoption is legal in the U.S.

> For more information on the *Child Citizenship Act*, see:
> **http://travel.state.gov/childcit.html**

To become a citizen, your child's passport (from his or her country of origin) will be stamped with USCIS Stamp I-551. You can then apply for a passport for your child (a passport will be your child's proof of citizenship). To apply for a passport, you need the following:

+ DSP-11, Application for a Passport;
+ two (2) identical photographs (2x2 inches in size);
+ the parents' valid identification;
+ certified adoption decree (with English translation, if necessary);
+ the child's foreign passport with USCIS Stamp I-551 or the child's Resident Alien Card; and,
+ the fee payment.

Readoption

Because United States courts are not required to legally recognize an adoption completed in a foreign country, it is a good idea to adopt your child in your state court, even if you have already completed an adoption process in the child's country of origin. At this time you will obtain a new birth certificate. This will ensure your child has an accurate birth certificate that is acceptable in the U.S.

Changes in Adoption Law

At the time this book was published, the U.S. was close to approving changes to international adoption law. The *Hague Convention on Intercountry Adoption* is an international document that provides procedures and rules for how international adoptions are handled and processed. If the U.S. does adopt these rules, there will be some changes to the way international adoptions are handled to ensure that the children placed for adoption are truly available. Some experts say the changes will complicate the international adoption process, while others say the changes will provide important protections for all involved in the process.

To read more about proposed changes in how international adoptions are handled and the effects of a change, see:

http://uscis.gov/graphics/services/HagueFS.pdf

Forms Checklist for International Adoption

❑ passports (if you will be traveling to your child)

❑ parents' birth certificates—3 copies

❑ marriage certificate—3 copies

❑ divorce decree (if applicable)—3 copies

❑ home study

❑ fingerprints

❑ criminal background check

❑ medical reports—2 copies

❑ reference letters

❑ form I-600A and/or I-600 Orphan Petition

❑ form I-864 Affidavit of Support

❑ form IR-3 or IR-4 to apply for a visa

International Agency Questionaire

Name of Agency_____

Name of Contact Person_____

Date of Interview_____

Questions:

❏ What countries do you have agreements with?_____
_____

❏ How many children have you placed from each of these countries in the last year?_____
_____

❏ How long have you worked with each country?_____
_____

❏ Do the overseas agencies you work with also work with other U.S. agencies?_____
_____

❏ Who works overseas for your agency?_____
_____

❏ How do babies come into the programs?_____
_____

❏ How long will the process take?_____
_____

❏ If parents must travel to complete the adoption, what arrangements and assistance do you provide for the trip? _____
_____

   ❏ Is a travel agency involved?_____
   _____

   ❏ Is an escort provided?_____
   _____

   ❏ Is a translator provided?_____
   _____

   ❏ Can the agency be reached by phone outside of business hours while we are overseas?_____
   _____

❏ What access is provided to the children overseas?_____

_____

❏ Can the agency provide referrals to Western doctors in the overseas country while we are there, should the need arise?_____

_____

❏ Are you licensed in this state?_____

_____

❏ How long have you been doing international adoptions?_____

_____

❏ If a parent turns down a child, can he or she adopt another child?_____

_____

❏ What kinds of services do you provide after placement?_____

_____

Chapter 8

Parent-Facilitated Adoption

A *parent-initiated adoption* is also sometimes called a *private* or *independent adoption*. The adoptive parents locate a birth mother on their own without help from an adoption agency. The reasons for doing this are often because the couple wants to adopt a newborn, the couple does not want to work with an agency, the couple wants more control over the process, or the couple wants more in-depth contact with the birth mother than is often allowed in agency adoptions.

While a parent-initiated adoption can offer a lot of freedom, it has some drawbacks. The main concern is that if you go through the adoption process without an agency involved, you may not be completely aware of all the laws and regulations you need to comply with. Additionally, there is always the chance that the birth mother will change her mind. While this does happen with agency adoptions, the likelihood increases when an agency is not involved to counsel and support the birth mother in making this decision. An agency can often provide an experienced hand that will guide your adoption and help you get over any bumps in the road.

On the other hand, a parent-initiated adoption allows you to do things your way, without having to apply to an agency or jump through their hoops. You locate a birth mother that you feel a connection with and you handle the process yourself (with help from your attorney).

Parent-initiated adoption is not permitted in Colorado, Connecticut, Delaware, Massachusetts, and Wisconsin. In these states you must use an agency for the adoption process. However, you can still locate a birth mother on your own and then have the adoption handled by an agency.

Adopting Independently with an Agency

Many parents who choose to locate a birth mother on their own use an agency to handle the actual adoption process itself. To do so, you need to interview agencies in your area and choose one that will handle a parent-initiated adoption. The agency will coordinate the home study, provide counseling, and work with your attorney to complete the adoption process. If you are comfortable working with an agency in this way, it can make the entire process go much more smoothly. There is an intermediary between you and the birth mother and you have someone handling the paperwork on your behalf.

For support with and information about private adoption, contact:

Families for Private Adoption
P.O. Box 6375
Washington DC 20015-0375
202-722-0338
www.ffpa.org

The agency will usually handle payment of the birth mother's expenses, so you need not pay them directly (it will be part of the costs you pay to the agency). However, you will have to pay an agency fee, which you would not pay if you handled the adoption directly with the birth mother.

How to Find a Birth Mother

There are several ways to go about finding a birth mother on your own. First, you may wish to talk to an attorney who is experienced in handling adoptions. Not only will the attorney help you understand the law and how you must go about contacting and reaching an agreement with a birth mother, but also, many experienced adoption attorneys have contact with birth mothers seeking adoptive parents for their babies. He or she may be able to help you find a birth mother.

Word of mouth is another excellent way to locate a birth mother. Tell your friends and family of your search and ask them to keep their ears open for you. Mention your search to coworkers and acquaintances. Some adoptive parents have business cards made up with their name, number, and a brief description along with words to the effect of *We can provide a loving home for your baby. Please call us.* Hand these out to friends and family and ask them to pass them along to anyone who might be interested. Give some to your gynecologist, family doctor, pastor, rabbi, and so on, if possible. Other couples create a letter to circulate to prospective birth mothers (this is often called a *Dear Birth Mother letter*) that describes you and your hopes to have a family.

> Get more information about birth mother letters at:
> **www.canadaaadopts.com/registry/mistakes.shtml**

Facilitator

Another option is to use an *adoption facilitator.* This is a professional who works to bring birth mothers and adoptive parents together. Facilitators are not licensed in most states and some states do not allow the use of facilitators. It is a good idea to speak with your attorney before approaching a facilitator. If you do decide to work with one, make sure you check references. Find out how many babies he or she has placed in total as well as in the last year. Make sure that you completely understand any fees involved as well as what the fees would be if a birth mother changes her mind. Only California, Connecticut, Florida, and Iowa have laws specifically permitting payments to an adoption facilitator.

> You can find a list of facilitators online at:
> **www.abcadoptions.com/facilitators/facilstate.htm**

The following areas do not permit the use of a facilitator:
- Alabama
- Colorado
- Delaware
- District of Columbia
- Illinois
- Kentucky
- Louisiana
- Maryland
- Massachusetts
- Michigan
- Nevada
- New Jersey
- New York
- North Carolina
- North Dakota
- Oklahoma
- Oregon
- Tennessee
- Texas
- Vermont
- Virginia
- West Virginia
- Wisconsin

Costs are usually less than private agency fees because the full range of services is not included in the contract. For example you would need to pay for the home study, medical exams, counseling, and so on separately.

Advertising

The most popular method employed by adoptive parents to find a birth mother is advertising. You may have seen classified ads in your local paper or in national papers. The following states do not permit advertising by prospective parents:

+ Alabama
+ California
+ Delaware
+ Florida
+ Georgia
+ Idaho
+ Kansas
+ Kentucky
+ Maine
+ Massachusetts
+ Nevada
+ North Carolina
+ Ohio
+ Washington

If your ad starts with the letter "A," it will be near the top of all adoption ads in the paper. Since most classified ads are short, you will want to spend a lot of time polishing your ad so it contains the most information in the clearest way. Most ads make references to a loving home, financially stable couple, friendly neighborhoods, and other positive factors. Mentioning your professions can help if they are prestigious or sound comforting (such as a doctor, a lawyer, a nurse, or a teacher). The cost of the ad depends on where you place it, but normal classified ad rates usually apply if you are advertising in newspapers. National papers charge higher rates than local papers. Compare the circulation of the papers to determine what prices are best—the higher the circulation, the more people the ad will reach. Read the classifieds in your local paper to see some ads and get a feel for how you want yours to look.

For tips about wording and placing an ad, visit: **www.library.adoption.com/Finding-an-Adoption-Situation/ Finding-Birthmothers-in-the-Classfied-**

Ads placed online are the newest way to locate a birth mother. Before you place an online ad, make sure you find out how many hits the site is receiving each month and ask for references. If you place an ad, you need to make sure your ad complies with all state laws, so be sure to consult with your attorney.

Do not underestimate the power of networking and getting the word out. Tell all your family and friends about your search for a baby and ask them to tell people they know. You might also consider creating a website that showcases your birth mother letter and has photos of you and your home.

Choosing a Birth Mother

Choosing a birth mother is a delicate process. When a birth mother contacts you, your first reaction might be to finalize things before she can change her mind. However, it is important to give yourself time and space to get to know her and to make this important decision. Make up a list of questions you want to ask a potential birth mother. You will not be able to ask her all of these questions the first time you talk, but you will have a written check-list of questions to ask as you have further conversations.

You must decide how comfortable you are with the answers to these questions. For example, if the birth mother smokes, you may wish to find someone else. If the birth mother gives you answers that conflict or that change over time, you may see a red flag. Try to get a sense of what the birth mother is like, what her life is like, and how serious she is about the adoption. You do not want to waste your time with someone who is not at all committed or who might just be trying to get money from you without fulfilling the agreement.

Write down the answers you get and discuss them with your adoption attorney. He or she will be able to guide you as to what kinds of problems to look for. It is easy to get emotionally invested too soon with a birth mother—the thought that this could be your baby can blind you to the warning signs. For this reason, it is important that you work carefully and closely with a professional who can help you see potential problems.

Contact with Birth Mother

Once you are in touch with a possible birth mother, it can be tempting to want to spend a lot of time talking to her and working things out. However, once you have a birth mother who calls you (she should always call you—you should never make the initial call because you do not want to create extra pressure and you must be careful to stay within your state's legal requirements), you need to tell her a little about yourself, find out a little about her (such as when her due date is, how her health is, and if the birth father is in the picture at all), and then have her call your attorney.

Your attorney is not able to call her (this creates pressure and she must enter the adoption of her own free will), so you need to stress to her the importance of calling your attorney herself. Your attorney will then proceed from there and make arrangements for medical exams, counseling, and for necessary paperwork. You will have many more opportunities to speak with the birth mother before either of you makes a decision about the adoption.

Payments

The average cost of a private adoption is about $13,000. The issue of payments involved in adoptions is a tricky one. It is unrealistic to expect a woman to place her child for adoption without any kind of financial assistance. However, laws about adoption payments were created to make sure that babies are not bought and sold. In most states, adoptive parents are expected to pay for the birth mother's medical expenses (this includes mental health counseling) during the course of her pregnancy. (See Chapter 3 for more information.) Payments are usually made through third parties—attorneys, facilitators, or agencies that are brought on board after the birth mother has been found.

If the birth mother has health insurance (and many do not) the expenses will be lower. The adoptive parents also handle the baby's expenses from birth. In some states, the law permits the adoptive parents to pay the birth mother's living expenses (basics like rent, utilities, food, and so on) during the last trimester of the pregnancy. Payments are usually permitted if they are *usual and customary* in the state. It is important that you check with your attorney before making any payments to the birth mother so that you are sure you are following your state's law exactly. Adoptive parents can also pay for the birth mother's attorney's fees if she employs an attorney. None of these payments are refundable if the birth mother chooses to keep the baby (except in Idaho, where they are reimbursable).

When you go to court to finalize your adoption, you will have to disclose to the court any payments you have made to the birth mother. For this reason, it is important that you remain within the allowable amounts in your state.

The following states specifically allow payment of birth mother's living expenses:

+ Arizona—must be court approved over $1000;
+ California—must be requested in writing by birth mother;

+ Connecticut—includes maternity clothes;
+ Florida;
+ Idaho—payments may be made up to six weeks after the birth, not to exceed $2000 without court permission;
+ Illinois;
+ Indiana—payments may be made up to six weeks after the birth, not to exceed $3000;
+ Iowa;
+ Kansas;
+ Louisiana—payments may be made up to forty-five days after the birth;
+ Michigan—payments may be made up to six weeks after the birth;
+ Minnesota—payments may be made up to six weeks after the birth;
+ Missouri;
+ Nevada;
+ New Hampshire—payments may be made up to six weeks after the birth;
+ New Jersey;
+ New Mexico—payments may be made up to six weeks after the birth;
+ North Carolina—payments may be made up to six weeks after the birth;
+ North Dakota—payments may be made up to six weeks after the birth;
+ Oregon;
+ South Carolina—payment may be made for a reasonable period of time;
+ Tennessee—payments may not be made forty-five days prior to birth or surrender or thirty days after without court approval;
+ Utah;

✦ Vermont;

✦ Virginia; and,

✦ Wisconsin—up to $1000.

Counseling

Before you agree to anything, it is essential that the birth mother attend counseling. An initial evaluation will help reveal any negative feelings she has about the placement. Ongoing counseling will help her deal with the inevitable emotions she will face as she goes through the pregnancy and delivery and the adjustment period afterwards. Your attorney can assist the birth mother in locating a counselor experienced in adoption. You will pay for the cost of this counseling.

Counseling can also be helpful for the adoptive parents. As you wait for your baby to be born, you will also face anxiety, doubt, and fear. A counselor can help you work through the process and stay focused on the goal of adding a child to your family.

Counseling should be part of your agreement with the birth mother. It is a warning sign if a birth mother is resistant to counseling. At the very least, you must have a psychological evaluation done so that you know what you are dealing with. There are some instances in which counseling might not be necessary, but in general, it is considered necessary for all adoptions. Counseling is usually done separately for adoptive parents and birth mother, but there are some instances in which going together can be helpful, particularly if there are issues you need to work out of if you are trying to create a plan for how you will have contact after the birth.

If your birth mother lives in your area, you can provide her a with a list of counselors and even offer to drive her there. If she lives far away from you, you can still put together a list of counselors in her area.

For referrals to counselors, visit the *American Psychological Association* at:

www.apa.org

Waiting for Your Child to be Born

When you use parent-initiated adoption, you are more closely in tune with what is happening with the birth mother as the pregnancy develops and you may have the opportunity to see or speak to her throughout the pregnancy. This relationship may be very close or not close at all. Each adoption is different and you will have to work within your comfort zone as well as that of the birth mother. Your attorney or adoption agency can be helpful intermediaries in this situation and can help communicate some basic rules for contact.

Some birth mothers and adoptive parents make arrangements for the adoptive parents to be present at the birth. You will need to work this out with your birth mother in advance. If you are present at the hospital, you will want to make sure the staff is aware you are the adoptive parents so that you can have access to the birth mother and baby. The birth mother will need to give her specific consent to this since the baby belongs to her until the placement occurs. If she does not consent, you have no right to see her or the baby.

Paperwork

As with any other adoption, the adoption is not finalized and complete until the waiting period is up, which varies depending on the state the child is born in. (See Chapter 3 for more information.) Any agreements you make with the birth mother before this are all subject to revocation of her consent to the adoption. While you and the birth mother will sign documents (that will vary by state) indicating that you consent to the adoption, this can all change if the birth mother changes her mind within the revocation period.

It is essential that you use an attorney to draft all the adoption documents. You will want to be sure that the papers you and the birth mother sign and present to the court are correct for your state and legally acceptable to the court. The birth mother must have her own attorney and cannot use yours. The court may scrutinize a parent-initiated adoption more closely than an agency adoption to be sure that state laws about payment and consent have been carefully followed.

NOTE: *If you and the birth mother live in different states, you will need to hire an attorney to represent you in each state. First choose an attorney in your home state. He or she will be able to locate an attorney in the other state to assist with the case.*

Once the waiting period concludes, the adoption is legalized and you become parents. (See Chapter 3 for more information about adoption paperwork and about birth certificates.)

Adjustment Period

After the adoption has been finalized in your state, the legal process is over for you, but the adjustment process will probably still continue. You will need to find a way to manage contact with the birth mother. Hopefully this was something you discussed and worked out with her while you were waiting for the birth, but do not be surprised if things do not go as planned. Some birth mothers who wanted regular contact may find it is less painful to get some distance and move on with their lives. Other birth mothers who thought they would want little contact may find they want more than originally thought.

Keep in mind that you are now the legal parent of this child and you are the one making the decisions. It is a good idea to try to be fair to the birth mother simply because this is what is right to do for your child, but you must make the ultimate decision about what is best for your child and what works for your family.

Choosing a Facilitator
Questionaire

Name of Facilitator _____

Date of Interview_____

Questions:

❏ How many adoptions have you placed in the last year?_____

_____

❏ Can you provide references?_____

_____

❏ How long have you been doing this?_____

_____

❏ How many clients do you work with each year?_____

_____

❏ How do you find birth mothers?_____

_____

❏ How do you evaluate birth mothers?_____

_____

❏ What is your success rate?_____

_____

❏ How many of your birth mothers change their minds?_____

_____

❏ What are your fees?_____

_____

Potential Birth Mother Questionaire

Name of Birth Mother_____

Date of Interview_____

Questions:

❑ Why are you placing this child for adoption?_____

_____

❑ How far along are you?_____

_____

❑ What is your due date?_____

_____

❑ Who knows about your pregnancy?_____

_____

❑ Who is the birth father?_____

_____

❑ Is he aware of the pregnancy?_____

_____

❑ Have you seen a doctor?_____

_____

❑ Who is your doctor?_____

_____

❑ Do you have any medical conditions?_____

_____

❑ Do you want an open adoption and if so, what do you mean
by that term?_____

_____

❑ What are you looking for in the adoptive parents?_____

_____

❑ Do you have a job?_____

_____

❑ What do you do?_____

_____

❏ Do you smoke, drink, or take any medication?_____

_____

❏ Are you taking prenatal vitamins?_____

_____

❏ What is your family medical history?_____

_____

❏ What is your ethnic heritage?_____

_____

❏ How old are you?_____

_____

❏ What education do you have?_____

_____

❏ Where do you live?_____

_____

❏ Who do you live with?_____

_____

❏ Are you in a relationship?_____

_____

❏ Do you have other children?_____

_____

❏ Have you placed any other children for adoption?_____

_____

❏ Have you talked with a counselor or adoption agency about
placement?_____

❏ What kind of support system do you have in place?_____

_____

❏ Can you provide photos of yourself and other family
members?_____

_____

❏ How long have you known about the pregnancy?_____

_____

Chapter 9

Adult Adoption

When most people think about adoption, they think about adoption of a child. In fact, it is possible to adopt another adult. There are various reasons why an *adult adoption* might occur. Some people develop very strong parent-child type bonds with people they are not related to. If their legal parents are deceased or they have broken ties with them, an adoption is a way to formalize the bond they feel with each other and also to provide inheritance rights.

Another common instance of adult adoption is when a man believes himself to be another person's biological parent, but it has never been proven and there is no other legal father. In these instances, it can provide closure for both parties and legalize a relationship they believe already exists. Adult adoption is also common in a stepparent situation. The stepparent may have wished to adopt the child but the other legal parent would not consent. Once the child becomes an adult, the adoption can occur and is a way to legalize the parent-child relationship that developed with the stepparent.

Adult adoption has also occasionally been used by gay and lesbian couples as a way to legalize a relationship where marriage is not permitted. The adoption gives the couple legal ties, including inheritance rights and the ability to make medical decisions for each other. Most gay couples find that this does not provide them with the type of legal bond they are seeking. There are other alternatives that work better, such as Vermont civil unions, domestic partnerships, and ongoing growth in gay marriage rights.

Evaluating the Need for Adult Adoption

If you are considering adult adoption, you need to first think about what your reasons are for the adoption. The emotional and psychological benefits can be worthwhile. Some people choose an adult adoption to provide a legal link so that they need not worry about *inheritance*. Inheritance issues can easily be dealt with by having a simple will drawn up, so this should not be used as the main reason for this type of adoption. Although you can use a will to direct your inheritance, dealing with survivor benefits is another matter. Only a legal child can receive survivor benefits or sue on behalf of a deceased parent.

Another reason for adult adoption is if a person has special needs. If a person who has special needs loses his or her parents, he or she may need someone else who can step in and fill that role for them. This would include being able to make medical and financial decisions for the person.

Restrictions

Not all states permit the adoption of adults. Alabama and Ohio allow this type of adoption only if the adoptee is permanently physically or mentally disabled. Ohio also permits adult adoption if the adoptee is a foster child or stepchild. Idaho and Illinois permit adult adoption only if there has been an ongoing parent-child relationship for a period of time.

Arizona, California, Connecticut, Delaware, Kentucky, Louisiana, Missouri, New Jersey, New Mexico, South Carolina, Texas, and Wisconsin do not specifically permit adult adoption, but do not ban it either. Colorado permits adult adoption only for adoptees between the ages of 18 and 21.

Massachusetts permits adult adoption, but requires that the adoptee be younger than the adoptive parent, unless an aunt, uncle, spouse, or sibling is doing the adopting. Virginia has a similar law, but allows adoption by aunt, uncle, or stepparent, or by anyone else for a good reason if the adoptive parent is fifteen years older than the person being adopted. Nevada also requires that the adoptee be younger than the adoptive parent. South Carolina requires that the adoptee has lived with the adoptive parent for at least six months while he or she was a minor.

Consent

Both the adoptee and the adoptive parent must consent to the adoption. There is no consent required by the adoptee's legal or biological parents.

Legal Procedure

If your state permits adoption of adults, a different set of forms is most likely used. Home studies and background checks are not required in most states, since the adult being adopted is presumed to be able to evaluate the situation on his or her own—although this may differ if the adoptee has mental disabilities. The legal process is relatively fast for normal adults since there is no need to wait for the intensive checking to be completed. A court date will be held and both the adoptive parent and adoptee will be present and provide consent to the adoption. If the adoptee has special needs, the court will appoint a *guardian ad litem* who will evaluate the situation and make recommendations to the court. The process will take longer when dealing with a person with special needs.

Effect of Adult Adoption

When an adult adoption is finalized, the adoptive parent becomes the adoptee's legal parent. The adoptee may no longer inherit from his or her biological parents (unless one of them is listed on the birth certificate as a second parent or unless a bequest is specifically made in a will). The adoptee also can no longer inherit from other biological relatives unless a will specifically provides for this. The new legal parents take the role of a parent in every way, which can mean making medical and financial decisions for a special needs adult.

Chapter 10

Single-Parent Adoption

Single-parent adoption is more commonplace than it ever used to be. Every state now recognizes that a good home does not depend on having two parents present and allows adoption by singles.

Considerations for Single-Parent Adoption

When you seek to adopt as a single, the primary concern that agencies and social workers will have is that you have a support system in place. Before seeking to adopt, give some thought to who will help you; who can provide child care; and, how you will provide role models of both sexes for your child. Family and friends provide excellent back up as well as opposite sex role models.

When making the decision to adopt as a single person, it is important to realize the weight of the decision. A child will be completely dependent on you. You also will carry the financial and emotional burden alone—as well as deal with all of the logistics of raising the child.

Before you adopt, it is important to carefully think through all the possible scenarios—how your child will be cared for while you work; how you will afford the additional expenses; who you will turn to for help; how you will continue to have a social life; who will care for your child should you die; and, so on.

Bias against Single Parents

While single-parent adoption is permitted in all states, some agencies and social workers continue to hold a bias against prospective single adoptive parents. If you encounter this kind of bias, it is best to confront it head-on and provide a lot of information for the agency or worker about your support system and deal with their concerns up front. There is often particular bias against single men seeking to adopt, based on misguided suspicions about pedophilia. Single men may have to work harder to convince agencies and social workers about their reasons for wanting to adopt, but have the same rights to adopt as anyone else. No one can turn you down for adoption simply because you are not married; however, other excuses may be used to discourage you. If you are confronting bias, it is a signal that you need to seek out another less judgmental agency.

For information and support, contact:
National Council for Single Adoptive Parents
P.O. Box 55
Wharton, NJ 07885
www.adopting.org/ncsap.html

There is also often an assumption that a single seeking to adopt must be gay. (See Chapter 11 for information about gay and lesbian adoption.) While you may be asked about your sexual orientation as part of the home study process, it should not matter what your orientation is as long as you have a lifestyle that is conducive to parenting.

Home Studies

You may need to work a little harder than married couples to get through the home study. You will need to show the social worker that you have thought through all the possibilities and have come up with a plan or with solutions to deal with them. Generally, it will be important to demonstrate a support network of family and friends who can step in to help. You should show that you have given thought to child care and that you know how to arrange your finances so that you can handle the extra expenses. You should also create a plan to take some time off when the adoption happens so you can bond with your child and ease the adjustment. Make it clear that you have planned this very well and that you feel secure in your ability to handle it. You will also need to show that you have a plan in place so that others are available to care for your child should you become ill, tied up at work, or have to go out of town. You should also mention that you plan to have a will drawn up that will name a guardian for your child.

Laws Governing Single-Parent Adoption

All states permit singles to adopt. However, there are a few catches. In Utah, where adoption by singles is permitted, anyone who is unmarried and cohabiting is not permitted to adopt. Florida does not permit adoption by anyone who is homosexual. Korea is currently the one foreign country that does not permit adoption of its children by singles.

Protecting Your Family

Single parents who adopt should consider purchasing disability insurance and life insurance to provide for their family's financial security. It will also be essential to execute a will naming a guardian for your child. You may wish to execute this will before your adoption is finalized. (There has been a case in which a woman had a fatal accident as she was returning home with her newly adopted child and since she had no will, the court had to decide on a guardian.)

Raising Your Child

With more and more people divorcing and singles adopting or having children without a partner, the single-parent family is no longer an oddity. Few people will give your adoption a second thought. However, there are some people who will simply not understand that your child does not have another parent. They will assume you must be divorced or not living with your child's other parent.

As you raise your child, you will encounter some bumps in the road. There is just one of you and you cannot be in all places at all times. Conflicts will come up, but if you have a support network in place, your child will be well cared for. Make sure that you leave room in your life for friends and for dating, if that is what you are interested in. You may be a parent, but you are still a person. You should be able to continue to work hard at your career, have fun, and spend some money on yourself. Parenting is not all about sacrifice.

Realize that although single parenting is easy for you to accept, it may not be easy for other people to accept. You may find yourself explaining more times than you wish that no your child does not have another parent and no, you are not widowed or divorced. As your child grows, spend some time explaining the different kinds of families and how you came to be a single parent.

Children of single parent families thrive and do just as well as children from families with two parents. In short, adopting a child on your own does not provide any particular roadblocks or problems for your child, unless you create them.

Chapter 11

Gay and Lesbian Adoption

In recent years, the laws about same-sex couple adoption have become more encompassing as more and more states have accepted gay couples as adoptive parents. There are several paths to consider when you and your partner want to become parents.

Single-Parent Adoption

If you are gay and single, your sexual orientation should not come into play with adoption. The information contained in Chapter 3 details the process and procedures you should follow. However, the information contained in this chapter will provide some specific information for a gay or lesbian person seeking to adopt.

Second-Parent Adoption

If one partner has a child (that is his or her natural child or is a child he or she adopted) and the other partner would like to adopt the child, a second-parent adoption procedure can be used. (See Chapter 4 for more information about second-parent adoptions.) There are some restrictions on same-sex, second-parent adoption, since it is not permitted in all states.

The areas that permit same-sex, second-parent adoption include:

+ California
+ Connecticut

+ District of Columbia
+ Illinois
+ Massachusetts
+ New Jersey
+ New York
+ Vermont

Other states have permitted some same-sex, second-parent adoptions, but do not have a clear cut policy. These states include:

+ Alabama
+ Alaska
+ Delaware
+ Georgia
+ Hawaii
+ Indiana
+ Iowa
+ Louisiana
+ Maryland
+ Michigan
+ Minnesota
+ Nevada
+ New Mexico
+ Oregon
+ Rhode Island
+ Texas
+ Washington

Florida completely disallows adoption by gays, as does Mississippi. Utah law does not allow unmarried people who are cohabiting to adopt.

Although the laws that permit second-parent adoption treat it as a separate process, in reality, gay couples are really adopting together. Yes, one partner must be the one to initially adopt the child and then the other partner can do a second-parent adoption, but these are just legal terms and processes and you should not get too bogged down with them. You are adopting together and you will parent together. There is no reason to think of it in any other way.

Read your state adoption laws at:
www.lambdalegal.org
or
www.hrc.org/familynet/adoption_laws.asp

Couple Adoption

Gay couples can adopt a child together, simultaneously, in Washington D.C., New York, New Jersey, Vermont, and California. Most other states have laws that are not clear on this issue.

However, this does not mean gay couples cannot adopt in most states. The best procedure to use in other states is a two-step adoption. In the first step, one partner adopts the child alone. He or she can use an agency or independent adoption—whatever method works best for him or her. Once that adoption is complete, then the other partner can seek a second-parent adoption of the child in those states that permit second-parent adoptions by gay partners.

International Adoption

Gay adoption is not permitted by any international country. However, this does not mean a gay single or couple cannot adopt. Single parent international adoption is possible if you are not open about your sexuality. If you are a couple, the child can then be adopted by the other parent via a second-parent adoption procedure.

For a list of countries with policies against gay adoption, visit:
www.travel.state.gov/adopt.html

Finding Gay-Friendly Adoption Agencies

To find a gay-friendly agency, talk to other same-sex couples who have adopted. Contact your local gay pride organization and ask for information about agencies they are aware of.

If you and/or your partner are seeking an agency adoption, it will be important to carefully question the agency about their policies regarding same-sex adoption. Listen not only to the official, written policy, but also to the nuances you pick up when talking to agency employees, in the literature you receive, and in all of your contacts with the agency. You want an agency that is comfortable with you and that will work to the best of its ability to place a child with you. If the birth mothers play a role in selecting adoptive parents, you will have a second barrier to deal with. Each birth mother will have her own preferences and opinions.

The *Human Rights Campaign* offers a database of gay-friendly adoption agencies at:

www.hrc.org/familynet/adoption_groups.asp

If the agency policy is accepting and welcoming, make sure you use one of the social workers employed by or recommended by the agency to avoid any potential bias when you go through the home study process. During the home study process it will be important to demonstrate that your relationship is solid and committed. If you have registered with any domestic partner registries, obtained a civil union or gay marriage license, or completed any affidavits for employers about your relationship (often required in order to access health benefits for a partner), it is important to share this information with your social worker. You should also mention a commitment ceremony or wedding, if you had one.

Public agencies are always a safe bet if your state has laws specifically permitting adoption by gays. There are always children available for adoption through public agencies, although they are usually not infants and may have special needs. (See Chapter 6 for more information about public agencies.)

> For information and support about gay parenting, contact:
> *Family Pride Coalition*
> P.O. Box 65327
> Washington, DC 20035-5327
> 202-331-5015
> **www.familypride.org**

Raising an Adoptive Child

Unfortunately, there is still discrimination against gays and their children. As you raise your child, you will need to be on the lookout for schools, camps, and organizations that will accept and welcome your child and your family. Keep an eye out for literature that refers to *parents* instead of *mothers* and *fathers*. Ask about GSAs (gay-straight alliances), school organizations that strive to support and include all students from all families. (The 1984 *Equal Access Law* held that if a school receives federal funds and has a limited open forum [meaning they allow other noncurriculum based groups to meet and use school resources], then the school cannot discriminate about which types of groups the school allows or supports.)

As you raise your child, you will find ways to talk to your child about being gay. Remember that being gay does not mean your child will be gay. Your child will have questions about your life, but for the most part it will feel completely natural to him or her. You and your child will probably encounter discrimination and ignorance. Spending time with other gay families or helping your child find support is important.

The *Gay, Lesbian and Straight Educational Network* can provide more information about school inclusiveness. Contact them at: 212-727-0135 or **www.glsen.org**

Your child will need role models from the opposite sex. Work with other gay or lesbian families to provide this kind of sup-port. You can also make sure your child spends time with straight family and friends so that he or she comes to know and love people of all types.

Help your child understand and deal with social reactions and help him or her understand the issues and your point of view by sharing books, such as those on the list created by *Children of Lesbians and Gays Everywhere* (COLAGE) at:

www.colage.org/pubs/books_for_kids.pdf

If you and your partner adopt your child together, you may encounter ignorance and unpleasantness at times. Many people are still unaware of the fact that gay couples can adopt children together and be legal parents together. You may have to offer proof to get someone to believe you—such as showing a birth certificate. Try to keep in mind that everything you do makes it easier for those gay couples or singles who come after you, so every bit of education or eye opening you do has meaning and purpose.

Chapter 12

Coping with Adoption

Adoption might be one of the bright moments in your life, but there will be bumps along the road as you work through the process. Working through the difficulties and disappointments might not be easy but will be worth it once you achieve your ultimate goal of adopting a child.

Dealing with Reactions to Adoption

While most people think of adoption as a good thing, there still seems to be a need to distinguish between adoptive children and biological children. Parents who adopt a child that does not resemble them will often be asked if the child is adopted. Some people go on to ask for details about the adoption. Each person who adopts has to make his or her own decision about how much information they are willing to share with other people about the adoption. You may feel that it is no one's business but yours and your child's. In fact, some adoptive parents choose not to discuss anything about the adoption with others and simply come up with an appropriate response that closes the subject for good.

Some parents decide that they are not going to discuss their child's origins with people they do not know. For instance, if you adopt a child from Korea and you are not Asian, people may come up to you and ask where your child is from, whether you knew his or her parents, and other details about the adoption. While these questions are often well-intentioned, they send a message to your child that he or she is different, that there is something strange in the way he or she entered your family, and that it is something to be questioned or discussed. Some parents choose not to discuss these details with other people and instead respond by explaining that they do not wish to discuss the private details of their family with other people.

You may also encounter people who assume that because you adopted, you had fertility problems. This is a misconception (so to speak!), since many people choose adoption without attempting to get pregnant.

What can be most disconcerting is the feeling that because you adopted your child, some people believe he or she is not really *yours* in the same way a biological child would be. People have a tendency to make a distinction between biological children and adopted children. You never hear anyone referring to someone's child as their biological child, but you quite often hear a reference to a person's adopted child. This is the kind of distinction many adoptive parents are working to change. Those who adopt know that it does not matter how a child comes to you. Your child is your child and how he or she joined your family is simply not important.

Dealing with Others Involved in Your Case

Because adoptions sometimes take longer than it seems they should, it is easy to become frustrated and annoyed with the people who seem to be holding it up—or at least not moving it along as quickly as you would like. While it is sometimes necessary to ask the tough questions and find out why there are delays, it is important to remember that you need to deal with the people involved with your adoption in a polite and friendly way. While adding a child to your family is a critical event for you, these people are simply doing their jobs—as rewarding as that may be—and they do not have the same sense of urgency, impatience, and frustration that you may feel.

While it is understandable that you may express your frustration and want solid answers about delays or problems, it is not a good idea to personally attack or argue with workers and officials. These people are the ones who are moving your case along. In general, you want to be cooperative when dealing with them and your goal should be to get them to like you if possible. Things move more quickly when there are good relations in place.

When dealing with an international adoption, it can be even more frustrating to have your fate held up by people you cannot even communicate with. When doing an international adoption, it is important that you work closely with your agency and that you are able to trust them to handle things for you. Make sure that if you travel to your child's country of origin, you know how to reach your agency at all hours if there is a problem or if you need help.

Dealing with the Waiting

Whether you are waiting through a birth mother's pregnancy, for a foreign country to match you with a child, or for a domestic agency to complete your home study, you will feel a level of anxiety and impatience. Remind yourself that adoption is a long process. Take things one step at a time and try to enjoy a sense of progress each time you move closer to the final resolution.

Joining an adoption support group can give you a place to talk about your feelings, offer you the chance to hear other people's experiences, and get advice. The waiting game can be hard on a relationship as well. You and your spouse or partner may find that you are on edge or more tense than usual. This too is normal. Remember that you are in this together and have the same ultimate goal.

You can find online adoption support at:
www.adoption.org/community

Dealing with Doubts

Adoption is a life-changing event. It is normal to experience doubts or have questions about the entire decision or process. The best way to deal with doubts or questions is head on. Look closely at your concerns. If you are doubting your ability to care for or love your adoptive child, you can rest assured that there will not be a problem once that child comes home to you. Counseling can be a big help in getting you to identify things you are worried or uncomfortable about and providing an outlet for you to work through the issues. If you are worried about parenting skills, consider taking a parenting class.

Doubts about the agency, birth mother, or social worker should be carefully considered. Express your concerns to the agency or to your attorney. Try to talk through these concerns and obtain reassurances to ease your mind. That being said, there are times when you just know something is wrong or not working. In those instances you should listen to your gut feelings.

Changing Your Mind

You can change your mind about the adoption any time until it is finalized. You may still be liable for expenses and fees up to that point. If you have serious unresolved doubts about the adoption or your situation has changed so that adoption is no longer a good decision for you, it is better to confront them now before you become an adoptive child's parent. The child you were going to adopt will be placed elsewhere, so you need not feel guilty.

Some families are lucky enough to unexpectedly become pregnant while attempting to adopt a child. The pregnancy does not affect your ability to adopt, unless *you* decide that it does.

Bonding with an Adopted Child

Many adoptive parents are worried about how well they will bond with their child. When a child becomes part of your life, your heart will open to make room for him or her. There is often the expectation that bonding is immediate—that once you see or hold your child you will immediately fall in love with him or her. Sometimes bonding is a gradual process, so do not be disappointed or upset if it takes you a little while to adjust to the new person in your life.

Read about attachment and bonding issues at:
http://attachment.adoption.com/index.php

Dealing with Adoption Disappointments

Occasionally adoption disappointments happen—a birth mother might decide not to place her newborn, a child that has been selected for you might have needs you feel you cannot meet, or something else may go wrong during the process to keep an adoption from happening. Birth mothers have the right to change their minds after the birth, so no adoption is certain until the court has made it legal. If you do experience a disappointment like this, it is important to give yourself time and room to deal with it. A particular dream that you had has ended. Some potential adoptive parents decide that they cannot try to adopt again after a disappointment, but most do try again. You might need some time or you might be able to move forward immediately to find a new child or birth mother. Adoption support groups can be a lifesaver when you are confronted with a disappointment, so seek one out if you need support or advice.

Support and assistance with failed adoptions is available at:
http://forums.adoption.com/f410.html

Chapter 13

Raising an Adopted Child

Once an adoption is complete, you can move on to the joy of being a family and raising your new child. However, raising an adopted child is not always the same as raising a biological child and there are some concerns and issues that may arise.

Celebrating Your Adoption

Once your adoption is complete, you will probably want to introduce your new family member to friends and family. Some people choose to send adoption announcements or hold a celebration or ceremony to welcome the child into the family. Many families treat an adoption as they would any other birth, with a baby shower.

As your child grows, you will need to think about how you will recognize the adoption. Some families hang special plaques in their home to commemorate an adoption. Other families celebrate their child's adoption day each year with a special celebration. Each family must make its own decisions about what they are comfortable with and what is the best way to mark this important event.

Breastfeeding an Adopted Infant

It is possible to breastfeed an adopted infant. Some mothers choose to breastfeed an adopted infant because of the known health benefits of breastfeeding or as a way to bond with the child, provide comfort, and create a physical connection to a child that you are not biologically connected to. For some women, it just feels natural to want to feed and nurture your child yourself.

The stimulation of nursing will cause a rise in prolactin, a hormone that stimulates milk production. However, adoptive mothers usually cannot produce enough milk on their own. Lactation aids can be used, providing supplementary formula to the infant while breastfeeding. Contact your pediatrician's office and ask to meet with a lactation consultant on staff. If your doctor is not supportive, find one who is.

For more information on breastfeeding for adoptive parents, contact the *La Leche League* at:
www.laleche.org

The Adoptive Breastfeeding Resource website at:
www.fourfriends.com/abrw

Talking to Your Biological Children about Adoption

If you have biological children, the adoption of a new brother or sister will be a time of excitement as well as anxiety. Many of the concerns and problems that arise are the same as those that occur when a child is added to the family through biological means. However, there are some concerns that are unique to the adoption situation. Young children may be terrified at the thought of a parent placing a child for adoption and may fear that this will happen to them. You will need to reassure your child that you are not placing any of your children for adoption and that this happens only in very unique circumstances.

Depending on the age of your biological children, there are different ways to discuss adoption. Getting a book about adoption can be one good way to explain it to your child. Another idea is to talk to you child about all the things parents do for their children—putting them to bed, changing diapers, feeding them, loving them, and so on. Then explain to your child that another thing parents do is bring the child into the world. Explain that children who are adopted have one set of parents who bring them into the world, but are unable to do all the other things a parent has to do, so the child gets adoptive parents who will do everything else for them for the rest of their lives. This will help prevent your biological child from worrying that you will one day not want him or her and place him or her for adoption.

It is important to make sure your child does not think of an adoptive child as one who was not wanted. Focus the discussion on the birth parents not being able to care for the child and give him or her everything he or she needs. If you refer to the adopted child as unwanted, you are setting the stage for your biological child to taunt your adoptive child.

Existing children may resent the attention an adopted child receives, especially if he or she has special needs or a situation that requires a lot of time and energy from the parents. It always takes work to help everyone adjust when you add a child to the family. Adoption situations are no different. Time, patience, and understanding are often the best remedies.

Raising Biological and Adopted Siblings

If you are raising a family created through birth and adoption, there is sure to be conflict—but there is conflict any time you have siblings, whether they are biologically related or not. It is essential you treat all of your children fairly and with respect and that they understand they are all equally part of the family. It is important to emphasize to children that all people are different and family members are different too. Your differences are what make your family special. Biological children take their cues from the parents. If you feel your adopted child is a full member of your family, they will as well.

If you are raising a child of a different ethnicity or from a different culture, you may wish to educate your adoptive child and any biological children (as well as yourself) about the history, culture, and traditions of the country or group of people. Doing so gives your adopted child a sense of identity; involves your family in his or her past; and, shows that you celebrate and appreciate who your child is and where he or she came from. You may also wish to spend time with families that have adopted children with similar backgrounds. (See Appendix A for a list of such organizations.)

Talking to Your Child about His or Her Adoption

Many parents tell their child basic information about his or her adoption from the very beginning. The story of how the child joined the family becomes a treasured story that is told over and over. When talking about adoption, most experts recommend that you emphasize that the birth mother or father made the placement decision out of love and concern. Some adoptive parents choose to emphasize that the child was meant to be part of this family, while de-emphasizing the idea that another family or mother did not want the child.

It is also helpful to point out that families are made in many ways—through birth, stepparenting, surrogacy, foster care, and so on. How the family was created is unimportant, but the fact that it exists is the primary fact. When you talk to your child about adoption, be sure to share how you felt and how important the adoption was to you and the entire family. Share details of the adoption, just as you would share details of a biological child's birth.

As your child grows older, you may be able to share more details about the adoption, such as the birth mother's name or facts about her. Being open with your child about the facts will help him or her feel comfortable with his or her own personal history.

As children become older, they want and need more details and often want to know specifics about their birth parents. As an adoptive parent, your role is to supply what information you can and offer support. If you have remained in contact with the birth parent, you will have a lot you can share. If you have no identifying information about the birth parents, your child can register with various adoptee groups to attempt to make contact with the birth parents. (See Appendix A for more information.)

The amount of information you share with your child at various points in his or her life will be up to you. In large part you should take your cues from your child. Offer information when he or she is interested in learning more.

> For more information about talking to your child about adoption, see:
> **www.adopting.org/talk.html**
> **www.rainbowkids.com/Articles/599talkingwithchild.htm**
> **www.adoptionconnection.org/NewsletterArticles/**
> **Talkingaboutadoption.html**

Keeping an Adoption a Secret

It is possible to keep an adoption a secret—after all, this is how adoptions used to be done. For the most part, it is not thought by experts to be a good idea anymore. Adopted children who are raised as if they are biological children may find out at some point that they were adopted. Discovering this kind of information can be very hurtful and disappointing. Think carefully about your reasons for wanting to keep the adoption a secret and how it can benefit your family. Weigh this against your child's need to know his or her own history and the sense of betrayal that is possible should the information ever be revealed.

Cultural Heritage

If your child has a cultural or ethnic heritage different than your own, you will want to share your own history and traditions with him or her. You may also want to try to incorporate some of his or her background into your family. Some adoptive parents who adopt internationally take many photos when they visit their child's country so they can later show him or her what it is like. Buying books and traditional clothing and games from your child's country is another way to help him or her connect with the past. Learn about the holidays and traditions from your child's country or ethnic group and celebrate them.

Consider joining an adoption support group for parents of children from specific countries such as
Families With Children From China at:
www.fwcc.org/welcome.html
Families with Children from Vietnam at:
www.fcvn.org

Your heritage will be important to your child as well and will become part of his or her own heritage. Your child will grow up eating your family's foods and celebrating your holidays. These things will belong to him or her just as they belong to you. However, some adoptive children may at some point feel as if participating in these things is somehow false for them. With a little encouragement and enthusiasm, you can let your child know that he or she is a very real part of your cultural line.

Medical Issues

When you adopt your child, you will receive some kind of medical history for him or her. This will include information about his or her health and may include a family history if available. It is impor-

tant to obtain as much information as you can. This may mean asking several times or paying for translations of documents from
another language if your adoption is an international one. The more
information you are able to gather, the better. While your child may
come to you in good health, he or she will need a detailed history
later in life and any information you can obtain will be helpful.
Some children come to adoption with very little medical history.
Your child still has every chance to grow up to be healthy.

Post Adoption Support

Adoption support groups are great ways to get information and
support while you are in the adoption process, but they are also
important in the post-adoption period. A support group can
help you and your child through the adjustments you face right
after an adoption, as well as with the ongoing issues that pop up
from time to time in an adopted child's life. Children can connect with other adoptive children through these groups. Also,
once you have gone through an adoption, you are in the perfect
position to offer help and encouragement to potential adoptive
parents who contact the group for information. (See Appendix A
for information on support groups.)

Finding Birth Parents

As your child matures, he or she may wish to learn more about his
or her birth parents, country of origin, or background. Some parents keep scrapbooks for their adopted children that includes the
birth mother letter they wrote, photos they took in the child's country of origin, photos of birth parents, adoption paperwork, or letters from birth parents. Depending on the type of adoption, finding your child's birth parent can vary in difficulty. Start with the
agency you worked with and contact information you had at the
time of adoption. You may need to hire an investigator to eventually find the birth parents.

Section II

Assisted Reproduction

Chapter 14

Understanding & Evaluating Reproductive Technologies

Reproductive technology has reached a point where there are many options available to help you become parents. These options have given couples a lot of freedom, opened the doors to wonderful new possibilities, and created many families. When you are considering using reproductive technologies to help you become a family, there are a lot of points to weigh and a lot of information to gather.

Understanding Your Condition

If you are considering assisted reproduction, it is important that you come into the process with a good understanding of why natural conception is not working for you and what conditions or problems have brought you here. Understand what your doctor thinks is realistic for you and your partner and what the odds are for you with the different types of treatment. Many times, doctors cannot give you a complete answer as to why you cannot conceive without assistance, but it is important to arm yourself with whatever knowledge is available.

In general, it is best to try the least invasive procedures first, if they provide real hope for you. This book talks mainly about fertility treatments that involve input from other people, but many couples are able to conceive using their own genetic material. There are many good treatments that are noninvasive, including drug therapies. Be sure to explore all of the options available to you and understand what could or could not work not before progressing to more invasive and complicated treatments.

What Technology Can Do for You

Technology can help you or your partner become pregnant; provide you with genetic material to create a baby if your body cannot do so itself; or, allow you to work with another woman to gestate your pregnancy. These options can seem staggering. Most people begin at the bottom of the totem pole with the least expensive and invasive options and work their way up to more expensive and complicated procedures.

What Technology Cannot Do for You

While technology can offer you new ways to become parents, it cannot change the basic facts of your circumstance. It cannot help you cope with the emotional effects of being unable to conceive on your own. Technology cannot erase basic biological facts. Technology can provide you with a baby, but it cannot always provide you with a baby that is genetically linked to both you and your partner. This can be a big stumbling block for many couples.

For many couples, it is possible to have a child that is a biological child of one of the parents, while using donor material for the other. This raises the issue of whether you and your partner are comfortable with all this implies—having a child who will resemble one of you but not the other; having a child who has an unknown or unidentified parent; and, the inevitable emotional fallout as you process these facts and live with them in the years to come.

Understanding Terminology

The assisted reproductive field is filled with acronyms for different types of procedures. Following are some definitions of these terms that will be used throughout the book.

ART—*assisted reproductive treatment.* This is the medical assistance you receive as you try to conceive.

GIFT—*gamete intrafallopian transfer.* Eggs (either belonging to the intended mother or obtained through donations) are retrieved from the ovaries and placed in the fallopian tubes with sperm. Conception occurs in a natural location, but allows physicians to carefully choose the genetic material available.

ICSI—*intra cytoplasmic sperm injection.* A single sperm is injected into an egg and the egg is then implanted into the intended mother.

IVF—*in vitro fertilization.* Eggs are fertilized with sperm outside out of the mother and embryos are implanted into her uterus.

IUI—*intrauterine insemination.* Ovulation is induced in the woman and sperm is then inserted into the uterus.

ZIFT—*zygote intrafallopian transfer.* Eggs are retrieved from the mother or donor and inseminated. The zygote or young embryo is then implanted into the fallopian tube.

Other terms you may come across include the following:

+ *gamete*. This refers to sperm or eggs—the building blocks of a baby.
+ *induced cycle*. Ovulation that is induced by medication.
+ *natural cycle*. Ovulation that occurs without medication or medical intervention.
+ *oocytes*. An egg before maturation.

For more information about options and available treatments, see:

www.fertilityneighborhood.com/content/treatment_options/ default.aspx

and

www.babycenter.com/refcap/preconception/fertilityproblems/ 4093.html

Finding Medical Professionals
You are Comfortable With

As you begin your journey into the world of assisted reproduction, the most important thing you can do is select doctors and clinics that you are comfortable with. The process you are entering is very stressful and emotional. If you are working with providers who are not sensitive to your needs or who you just feel uncomfortable with, the entire process will be more difficult for you.

The first place to start is with your OB/GYN. Get a referral to a fertility specialist. If you are not happy with that referral, ask for another. If there is a medical school in your area, call them and ask if the school is involved in a clinic in your area. Talk to other couples you know who have used assisted reproduction about what doctors and facilities they have used.

Before visiting a specialist or clinic, call and ask if the providers are board certified or board eligible in gynecology and obstetrics as well as in *reproductive endocrinology*. Fertility specialists should be certified in both of these areas. If the clinic has an IVF lab, ask if it is accredited by the College of American Pathologists (whether or not you plan on using IVF). All labs of any kind must be accredited under the federal *Clinical Laboratory Improvement Amendment* (CLIA). Ask if the physicians are members of the American Society of Reproductive Medicine. Most reputable clinics also have the following specialists on staff:

- ✦ reproductive immunologists;
- ✦ embryologists;
- ✦ reproductive urologists;
- ✦ andrologists; and,
- ✦ genetic counselors.

When meeting with a medical provider, there will be much information you need to gather from him or her. Use the checklist on page 163 to help the process move smoothly.

Success Rates

When you interview clinics, it is important to ask about *success rates*. This will let you know how successful the clinic is at producing pregnancies. The most important success rates are the number of take-home babies per year and the number of live babies born per cycle. (The number of pregnancies can be a deceiving statistic because many may fail early in the pregnancy.)

Keep in mind that some clinics may not have high success rates because they focus on difficult-to-treat problems or because they use last ditch methods that may be a couple's only hope. Make sure you understand why a clinic's numbers are what they are.

> You can check a clinic's success rates online at:
> **www.cdc.gov/needphp/drh/arts/index.htm**

Your Right to ART

Fertility clinics cannot turn you away because of a disability or discriminate against you because of your race or ethnic background. At the time this book was written, a case was being heard in Colorado about a blind woman who was required to show a clinic that she was able to care for a child before they would continue her IVF treatments. The court will consider whether the *Americans with Disabilities Act* prohibits this kind of discrimination. Clinics that receive federal funds may also violate the *Rehabilitation Act* if they treat those with disabilities differently than other patients.

Initial Visit

When you visit a fertility specialist, it is important to bring medical records, test results, and reports with you. Both partners (if you are part of a couple) should be at the first visit so that both can meet the doctors and ask questions. Ask yourselves if you feel comfortable with the people you meet there and with the general atmosphere. You also need to be frank with yourselves about what you can afford. Try to get clear answers about success rates. Evaluate what you are told with a critical eye.

Setting Limits

Most couples enter the world of assisted reproduction slowly— first with fertility drugs and then gradually moving on to other procedures. When you first begin to work with medical assistance to get pregnant or have a child, it is important to have a frank discussion with your partner about what types of medical assistance you are comfortable with. This is not a topic that normally comes up in most marriages, but once you begin to work with fertility specialists, a whole world of possibilities opens before you. You may not know how your spouse feels about sperm donors, egg donors, and surrogates.

Realize that what you think you know about your feelings and preferences now may change. If you move through different procedures with no success, you may feel that that the desire to have a child is more urgent than any objections you might have had earlier to certain types of fertility assistance.

Privacy

You and your partner will also have to make some choices about who you will tell about your ART procedures and what information you are willing to share with family, friends, and so on. You are not obligated to tell anyone, but most couples find they need the support that friends and family can provide.

Because ART procedures are medical procedures, they are protected by the *Health Insurance Portability and Accountability Act* (HIPAA). All of your records are confidential and cannot be shared without your permission.

Coping with the Medical and Clinical World

It is important to understand that while conceiving or creating a child is to you the most important thing in the world, you are another file to the clinic. That is not to say that you will not work with some very caring individuals who are sensitive to what you are feeling and the roller coaster you are riding. However, it is important for you as a patient and as a client to realize that your care providers are working in a clinical and detached way. At some point you may feel frustrated by this schism that lies between you.

Always try to be clear about your questions, comments, and problems when speaking with your care providers. If possible, try to be as unemotional as possible. Get as much information as you can from your providers before making important decisions.

Another consideration is the time commitment many ART procedures require. For some, such as insemination, the time requirement is minimal. Others, like IVF, have a significant time commitment that includes very frequent visits to the clinic. The geographical location of your clinic will determine just how great your time commitment will be. If you are traveling long distances to get to the clinic, it will be a greater burden than if the clinic is in your city. You may be able to take time off from work for your medical care. (If you qualify for coverage under *the Family and Medical Leave Act* (FMLA), you can take up to twelve weeks of unpaid leave for your own medical problems or to care for a family member.)

Also be aware that although you are dealing with doctors, you are still dealing with many legal issues. Do not assume that your medical expert is a legal expert. Get clarification from your own attorney on all contracts and legal documents you are asked to sign. When you are eager to conceive, it is easy to simply just sign so you can get things moving. However, in the long run, it is best to make sure you completely understand all the documents and their legal implications before you sign anything.

Your Rights as an ART Patient

This may be the first time in your life you have had to seek serious medical intervention. It is important to know what your rights are.

WHO IS THE PATIENT

Most people enter ART with a partner or spouse. When you approach the treatment with a partner, it feels to you as if both of you are the patient, since you are trying to create a child together. While your doctors may talk to you both together and treat you the same way, only the person who is receiving medical treatment from the provider is the patient. Because of privacy laws, if a woman is the one receiving treatment and her husband calls the clinic to get a test result or ask a question, the clinic is not supposed to release the information to him.

The way around this is to sign a release form that will be kept in your file. This will authorize the clinic to speak to both of you about any treatment, test results, or procedures at any time. Your clinic will have a form they will want you to complete, but they may not offer it automatically—you will probably have to ask for it. Giving your partner access to your treatment will help make this a joint venture and will also allow you the convenience of not having to make every phone call yourself.

INFORMED CONSENT

When you receive medical treatment, you must provide informed consent. This means that you must agree to the treatment after all the risks and benefits have been explained to you. Fortunately, in ART, your care providers will probably spend a lot of time talking with you about treatments, risks, and possible outcomes. If at any point you feel you do not have enough information to make a decision or if you feel confused about something, speak up and ask for more information. Always be sure to ask about risks and possible outcomes for you as well as for your child.

It is also important that you take the time to educate yourself about your condition and treatments. Spend some time doing Internet searches and reading articles so that when you see your provider, you are armed with some knowledge and are better able to ask questions. (See the resources provided in the Appendices for further information.)

Second Opinions

You always have the right to a second opinion and most insurance companies will pay for one. A second opinion is a good idea when you have been given bad news or when an invasive treatment is recommended. Do not ask your current doctor for a recommendation about who to see—he or she is likely to send you to someone with a similar viewpoint. Instead contact your insurance company and ask for names of other specialists or contact the national organization for the type of specialist you are seeing.

Refusing Treatment

You have the absolute right to refuse medical treatment and can walk out of any doctor's office, clinic, or hospital at any time. Refusing treatment is sometimes referred to as leaving *AMA* (against medical advice). You can change your mind about treatment, decide you want a second opinion, or feel that you need more time to think about something.

The one caveat that is involved with ART is that women are at the mercy of their cycles, so if you are scheduled for an IVF treatment but need time to think about it, you may miss your window of opportunity for that month. Additionally, if you have medical insurance that is paying for your care, and you refuse a recommended treatment, the insurance company may not pay for any complications or problems that result from your refusal of treatment.

Experimental Treatments

Because the ART field is constantly evolving, there may be new treatments available to you that have not been fully tested, proven, or reviewed. If you are considering an experimental treatment, find out what other options you have and compare them and their success rates with the experimental treatment. Some couples go to experimental treatments when everything else has failed, while others are anxious to try new things that may have better or faster results than more traditional treatments.

Educate yourself about the treatment—its costs, its risks, and its benefits. Ask a lot of questions and get information about what kind of testing it has undergone and what bad results have occurred. Find out how experienced the practitioner is with the treatment. Get information about costs up front. Your insurance company is unlikely to pay for experimental treatments, but it cannot hurt to ask. Some experimental treatments are funded by universities or other groups that reduce or remove any cost to you.

Making Time for ART

ART requires a time commitment from you. You must take drugs, have regular appointments, and make room in your life for the emotions that the drugs and procedures bring with them. It is not a small commitment. As you begin the ART journey, the commitment may be small, but the farther you go, the bigger the commitment becomes. It can be difficult to juggle a job with this focus.

If you work for an employer with fifty or more employees, you are probably eligible for the *Family and Medical Leave Act* (FMLA). This federal law allows you to take unpaid time off to care for yourself or a family member—up to twelve weeks per year. This time can be crucial if you have used up sick days and vacation time and still need to take more time off to travel to a clinic or to receive treatment.

Coping with ART

The decision to use ART can be a difficult one for many couples. Couples often come to ART after months or years of trying to conceive on their own. Making the decision to use ART is very emotional. It requires you to admit, at least to yourselves, that you need help and intervention. It can be truly devastating to realize and admit that you cannot conceive a child on your own. Taking what is a very private decision—the decision to make a baby—and having it become clinical, medical, and something that is discussed and evaluated can be painful. Many couples coming to ART do so with heavy hearts and a feeling of failure or worthlessness. It is important to understand that everyone needs a little help sometimes. The advances and technologies that are available today are truly miraculous and there is no reason to feel bad about needing them.

Realizing that you need assistance brings out powerful feelings and fears. Be open with your partner in discussing these feelings. Seek out counseling if you have difficulty coping with your feelings.

It is also important to note that infertility treatments can be very stressful on a relationship. Make time in your lives to enjoy each other, keep your relationship alive, and remember that it is important to express physical affection to each other when you want to—do not give up your spontaneity even though you may have to submit to some clinical schedules.

While it is hard to do, it is important to make sure that your treatment does not become your life. You had a life before you started trying to conceive and it is important that you keep it alive. Whether or not you are able to conceive a child, you must continue to develop your interests, further your career, and spend time with family and friends.

Weighing Technology against Adoption

There comes a point, once you have not been successful with fertility drug treatment, that you must choose a path. You must decide whether you want to pursue becoming a family through adoption or becoming a family through assisted reproduction. It is important to understand that no decision you make at this crossroad has to be the final word. It is possible to pursue both options at the same time and then, if one works, give up on the other. It is also possible to begin down one path only to change your minds and pursue the other choice. In other words, you are not making a final, irrevocable decision no matter what you start to do.

Some couples simply know which path they will pursue. Others need to think about the possible outcomes, financial costs, and emotional costs of both choices. There is no right or wrong answer.

Weighing the Use of Donors

When you enter into ART, you probably do so planning to use your own genetic material to conceive a child. But some couples are unable to do so and must use donor material. Choosing to use donor material involves an acceptance of what you are giving up. You are giving up your dream of having a child that is genetically related to you and your partner.

Many couples are able to have a child that is genetically related to one of them, but not the other. In this instance, you and you partner must be able to live with this knowledge. Some couples experience real problems over this. Seeing your wife carry a child that another man's sperm helped to create or carrying a baby that was created with another woman's egg can be a difficult burden. Some people feel jealous of the parent who will be genetically related, resentful that they are unable to genetically participate, or worried that somehow the child will not be as much theirs.

It is very important to consult with a counselor when making these decisions. Conceiving via ART can be a long and arduous journey. You could be carrying this pain for a long time. It is important to resolve these feelings, because if you do successfully conceive, you want to be able to parent with a loving and open heart.

Ethical Considerations

Depending on which ART you use, you may be faced with decisions that are ethical as well as practical. These can include what you will do with extra eggs that have been harvested or frozen embryos that you have not used. Once you have reached the decision that you will not be using this material, you are faced with a choice of what should happen with it. These decisions are highly personal, but boil down to three options—donate the genetic material to another couple/person who can use it; donate it to research; or, have it destroyed. Each option involves personal, religious, moral, and emotional issues. There are no laws governing what should happen to this material, but there can be disputes between couples about how to dispose of this material.

Financial Issues

The financial impact of the procedures you choose to use will probably be a large part of your decision-making process. While some procedures, such as insemination, are relatively inexpensive, others, such as IVF and surrogacy, are extremely expensive. What you can afford will probably have an impact on what path you choose to follow.

In most states, insurance companies are not required to provide coverage for infertility procedures. However, coverage is normally provided for diagnosis and treatment if there is an underlying medical cause for the infertility, such as endometriosis.

To determine if you have coverage for infertility treatment, ask your employer for a copy of your health insurance policy contract.

If your contract does not specifically exclude infertility treatment, then it is covered. If it mentions infertility treatments, read it carefully to see what, if anything, it does cover. It might, for example, cover diagnosis of infertility problems, but not actual treatment.

If your policy appears to provide coverage, but payment is denied for a treatment you or your spouse undergo, you can appeal the decision. Check your contract for details on how this is done. Denials are usually made because infertility is not an illness, the treatment was not medically necessary, or because the procedure or treatment is experimental. None of these are valid reasons for denial of coverage. A letter from your doctor is a helpful piece of evidence to use in an appeal.

Additionally, you may be able to prove that the denial of coverage violates the *Americans With Disabilities Act*. A 1998 Supreme Court case, *Kraul v. Iowa Methodist Medical Center*, held that infertility meets the requirements of the ADA. You need to speak to your attorney to discuss this option.

INSURANCE COVERAGE

The following states are currently the only ones that mandate insurance coverage for infertility.

Arkansas. HMOs are exempt from this law. Coverage for IVF with a two-year history of infertility or medical conditions causing it. Coverage is provided only if a patient's eggs are being fertilized by her husband's sperm. There is a lifetime cap on these benefits.

California. Coverage if infertility of one year or infertility creating medical conditions exist. GIFT is covered, but in vitro is not mandated for coverage. Coverage is required to be available (meaning there is an extra cost), but is not required to always be included in policies.

Connecticut. Coverage must be available, but does not have to be included in policies unless chosen. Includes diagnosis, treatment, and in vitro. Available for women who have been infertile for one year.

Hawaii. Provides a one-time-only in vitro benefit if there is a five year infertility history and the patient's eggs are fertilized with her spouse's sperm.

Illinois. Diagnosis and treatment are provided after one year infertility. A wide varieties of treatment is covered including IVF, GIFT, and ZIFT.

Maryland. Coverage is required for IVF, but HMOs are exempt. The patient's eggs must be fertilized with the spouse's sperm.

Massachusetts. Diagnosis and treatment are covered for women who have been unable to get pregnant in a one-year period. Includes insemination, IVF, GIFT, ZIFT, and other treatments. Coverage for surrogacy and cryopreservation is optional.

Montana. HMOs must provide coverage for infertility, but the law is vague as to what this entails.

New York. Covers the diagnosis and treatment of infertility, but does not cover IVF.

Ohio. HMOs must provide coverage for infertility. There is a $2000 cap if the infertility does not have a stated medical cause.

Rhode Island. Provides coverage for diagnosis and treatment of infertility.

Texas. Provides coverage for diagnosis and treatment including IVF. The patient's eggs must be fertilized by the spouse's sperm.

Singles and Assisted Reproduction

There is nothing unusual about being a single parent and it is becoming more common for singles to seek a child through assisted reproduction. As a single person, your primary concern should be finding a doctor or clinic that has no prejudice against singles becoming parents. Be up front about your single status and pay careful attention to how this news is received. There are some professionals who will make you feel more comfortable than others. The bottom line however, is that you have every right to pursue becoming a parent using any technology that works for you.

As a single who is considering becoming a parent, it is important that you think beyond conception and have a plan for how you would raise a child on your own. You need to have a good support system in place (friends and family) to help you when necessary. You must also be prepared for the ignorance and meanspiritedness from other people that you may encounter as you raise a child on your own. Single parents must also think about the financial implications of their decisions and how they will afford to raise a child on their own. It is best to have a plan for how you will raise your child before you begin assisted reproduction.

Being Gay and Using Assisted Reproduction

With the *gayby boom* of recent years, it is becoming more common for gay couples to become families using assisted reproduction. As with singles, you will find that some providers are more friendly to you than others. This should be an important clue to you. Try to work with clinics or providers who welcome gays whenever possible.

Note: *No matter what method you use to become a parent, you will need to use a second-parent adoption procedure to make the nonbiological parent legal. (See Chapter 4 for more information about second-parent adoptions.)*

For information about gay surrogacy options, visit:
www.growinggenerations.com

HIV and Assisted Reproduction

It used to be thought that a person with HIV should not use ART because of the risks involved to the other partner. It was feared that if the person providing the sperm is HIV positive, there would be a potential danger of contracting the virus to the woman carrying the pregnancy. New techniques that allow *sperm washing* have substantially reduced these risks. The key in any ART procedure involving HIV is complete disclosure. For example, if you are using a surrogate and the partner providing the sperm is HIV positive, it is important that the surrogate know this and be fully informed of any risks involved.

Dealing with Risks

Because you are considering cutting edge medical technology, it is important that you come to a clear understanding of the risks posed to you and your partner, as well as to your possible children. Medical risks should be discussed thoroughly and completely with your medical care providers. Do not allow your providers to assume you understand risks. Ask to have them spelled out. There are risks of infection and other problems from surgical procedures, as well as risks posed by fertility drugs used to stimulate ovulation, by pregnancy itself, and by other procedures you may encounter.

In addition to medical risks, you also face legal risks. When you are dealing with your own genetic material, the legal implications are not as great. However, when you begin to consider and use procedures that involve donated eggs, sperm, or zygotes (embryos), the legal risks become much larger.

It is imperative that you work closely with a reproductive rights attorney who has experience reviewing and drafting contracts for donations and surrogacy. Do not assume you can do this on your own. This book is designed to point out the important issues, considerations, and questions that should come up, but is not designed to allow you to do it yourself. Because you are dealing with your legal rights as a parent, you want an expert on your side.

NOTE: *To find a reproductive law attorney, contact your local or state bar association for a referral.*

Fertility Specialist Questionaire

Name of Specialist_____

Date of Interview_____

Questions:

❑ Where did you go to medical school and complete your residency?_____

_____

❑ How many years have you been a fertility specialist?_____

_____

❑ How many reproductive endocrinologists are on staff?_____

_____

❑ Will we work with you or several doctors?_____

_____

❑ Is there someone on call after hours?_____

_____

❑ Are you affiliated with a hospital?_____

_____

❑ What insurance plans do you accept?_____

_____

❑ Are payment plans an option?_____

_____

❑ How much will the proposed treatment cost?_____

_____

❑ What does that include?_____

_____

❑ What is your practice's number of take-home babies (babies that are born and go home with their intended parents)?_____

_____

❑ What treatments and services do you offer?_____

_____

❑ Can you provide referrals should we require other treatments?

_____

(continued)

❏ What support services do you offer?_____

_____

❏ What is your rate of live babies per cycle?_____

_____

❏ Is your lab accredited by the American College of Pathologists or the Joint Commission on Accreditation of Health Care Organizations?_____

❏ Do you report results to the Centers for Disease Control (CDC)?_____

_____

Chapter 15

Insemination

Insemination is a procedure in which sperm is inserted into a woman's body to attempt conception. There are a variety of ways insemination can occur. The simplest way is to use the male partner's sperm and insert it through the vagina. The insemination process is used so that the sperm can be sorted and the most viable sperm can be used.

When using sperm that comes from the male partner, the legal issues and problems are minimal. The couple is receiving medical assistance with their own genetic material. This chapter focuses on the issues surrounding the use of *donor sperm*, which is sperm that does not belong to the partners of a potential single mother.

Laws

There are no laws prohibiting the use of insemination by married or unmarried couples or by singles, so anyone is free to pursue this option. Before choosing donor insemination, it is important that a couple knows the cause of their infertility and their chances of pregnancy without donor insemination.

When a woman who is married gives birth, the child is legally her husband's. So if a married couple uses a sperm donor, the husband is the legal father and no steps are necessary to ensure this. Some states require the husband to consent in writing to the insemination.

The areas that do not require the husband's consent include:

- ✦ Arizona
- ✦ Delaware
- ✦ District of Columbia
- ✦ Georgia
- ✦ Hawaii
- ✦ Indiana
- ✦ Iowa
- ✦ Kentucky
- ✦ Louisiana
- ✦ Maine
- ✦ Maryland
- ✦ Massachusetts
- ✦ Michigan
- ✦ Mississippi
- ✦ Nebraska
- ✦ New Hampshire
- ✦ North Dakota
- ✦ Pennsylvania
- ✦ Rhode Island
- ✦ South Carolina
- ✦ South Dakota
- ✦ Tennessee
- ✦ Utah
- ✦ Vermont
- ✦ West Virginia

In the following states, laws remove any rights of donors:

- ✦ Alabama
- ✦ California
- ✦ Colorado
- ✦ Connecticut
- ✦ Idaho

+ Illinois
+ Kansas
+ Minnesota
+ Missouri
+ Montana
+ Nevada
+ New Hampshire
+ New Jersey
+ New Mexico
+ North Dakota
+ Ohio
+ Oregon
+ Texas
+ Virginia
+ Washington
+ Wisconsin
+ Wyoming

Types of Sperm Donors

There are two types of sperm donors—known and unknown.

KNOWN DONORS

A *known donor* is often a friend or family member of the couple or potential single mother. Using a known donor has advantages and disadvantages. The main advantage is you know exactly where the sperm came from, you know what the person's traits are, what his personality is like, and details about his medical history. You also have the ability to have ongoing contact with him after the pregnancy so that the child can someday meet and possibly have a relationship with him. Another advantage of postpregnancy contact is that you will have access to any medical information that comes to light after the insemination—for example, if the donor is diagnosed with diabetes or heart disease.

The disadvantages of a known donor are the emotional complications that can ensue. If the donor is a family member or close friend, the parents could come to resent his presence in the child's life or the donor could come to feel resentful about his small role in the child's life. Knowing the donor and having contact with him could cause confusion for the child (although in most cases this is not a huge issue—nontraditional family ties are not so unusual these days).

If you use a known donor you should still enlist the assistance of fertility specialists and clinics who can make sure the procedure is done appropriately and can put some safeguards in place. Even though you know the donor, you will want to be sure his or her sperm is tested for disease. Certain testing can take several weeks.

Some women or couples choose to do home inseminations. While the cost can be greatly reduced, the effectiveness may be decreased. If you do choose to do your own, make sure you use an insemination agreement. (See Appendix C for a sample agreement.)

For information on home insemination, visit:

http://homeinseminations.homestead.com/index.html

or

www.fertilityplus.org/faq/homeinsem.html

It is important for legal reasons as well as medical reasons to have the insemination performed by a physician. In some states, the rule about the married woman's husband being the legal father of a child produced through insemination only applies if the insemination was performed by a licensed physician.

Additionally, it is important that all the parties involved in the insemination procedure—the woman, the donor, and the woman's partner if one exists—obtain counseling. This will not only help the parties work through any problems they have with the procedure, but also will help ensure that problems will not appear in the future. Counseling ensures that everyone involved is certain about the decision and is emotionally able to handle its repercussions.

Agreements with Known Donors

Even though you have some kind of relationship with the donor, it is essential that you sign a legally binding insemination agreement. (See Appendix C for a sample Insemination Agreement.) It is important that you use a reproductive law attorney to draft an agreement that will meet the requirements of your state.

The agreement will have the donor give up all rights to custody or visitation with the child. This is essential so that he does not later change his mind and decide to seek custody. The woman receiving the sperm gives up all rights to seek anything from the donor, including child support.

If the woman receiving the donation has a partner, it is important that the partner sign the agreement and indicate his or her consent to the procedure as well. If the partner is her husband, this will further ensure that the child will be legally his. Information about nonmarried partners is provided later in this chapter.

UNKNOWN DONORS

Unknown donors are generally located through a *sperm bank*. Sperm banks pay donors for their sperm and carefully screen donors and their sperm for medical conditions and disease.

Certain states specifically require HIV screening of donor sperm. These states include:

+ Arizona
+ California
+ Connecticut
+ Delaware
+ Florida
+ Idaho
+ Illinois

+ Indiana
+ Iowa
+ Kentucky
+ Louisiana
+ Maryland
+ Michigan
+ Montana
+ North Carolina
+ North Dakota
+ Ohio
+ Oklahoma
+ Rhode Island
+ Virginia
+ West Virginia
+ Wisconsin

Note: *If your state does not specifically require HIV screening, you will want to be sure your clinic does it anyway.*

The sperm is frozen and preserved until testing is complete. The sperm bank makes sure that donors and the women who receive the donations receive counseling to help them cope with the decision. The woman using the sperm is charged a small fee—often between $200 and $400 for the sperm, not including the cost of the insemination procedure.

Sperm banks offer profiles of donors that include medical history, ethnic background, physical attributes, mental abilities, personality traits, and photos. Clients of the sperm bank can choose a donor that is physically similar to them in some way or who meets other criteria they have.

There is no government regulation of sperm banks in the U.S., although four states do license sperm banks: California, Maryland, Massachusetts, and New York. Some sperm banks are accredited by the *American Association of Tissue Banks* (AATB) but most are not. Additionally, the *American Society of Reproductive Medicine* (ASRM) has guidelines that the banks should follow. Some banks may say they meet or exceed the AATB guidelines, but this does not mean they are actually accredited by AATB, so be sure to pin this down. State health departments also offer certification of sperm banks, but you should be most concerned with AATB certification.

> Contact the *American Association of Tissue Banks* at:
> **www.aatb.org**
> and
> the *American Society of Reproductive Medicine* at:
> **www.asrm.org**

The facility should have guidelines that provide for:

+ obtaining a complete medical history from the donor;
+ personal interviews with all donors;
+ freezing sperm for six months to allow for complete testing of the donor and to do freeze tests on the sperm;
+ careful recordkeeping;
+ tracking of the number of pregnancies per donor;
+ limiting of the number of pregnancies per donor;
+ physical exams and blood tests for all donors for many diseases including HIV, Tay Sachs, Sickle Cell, etc.;
+ medical history going back four generations whenever possible;
+ genetic and chromosomal analysis;
+ ruling out mental health issues;
+ shipping of sperm using nitrogen;
+ the use of cryoprotectants that do not use chicken egg extract (due to possible allergies); and,
+ set minimum number of sperm per sample.

The sperm bank will provide the donor agreement and will ensure that both you and the donor are protected from future problems with custody and support. However, it is a good idea to have your own attorney read any agreement you are asked to sign.

Donors are not notified when their sperm is used, so they are very distant from the insemination process. Donors are paid a small amount for each donation they provide.

If you are ordering sperm from a sperm bank for home insemination, the sperm bank requires a physician's authorization to release it because donor sperm is considered a medical substance. Thus, it is necessary to see a doctor and have him or her agree to or approve your plans for home insemination through a sperm bank.

Legal Parents

As previously mentioned, when a married woman receives donor sperm and the procedure is performed by a physician, her husband is the legal parent of the child. If a donor agreement is used, the sperm donor has no rights to the child and cannot be held liable for support.

If an unmarried heterosexual couple uses insemination, the male partner will need to legally adopt the child after the birth using a second-parent adoption process. (See Chapter 4 for more information.) The mother will be the only legal parent of the child until this point. The donor's right will be terminated by the donor agreement.

If a single woman uses insemination, she is the sole parent of the child. The donor's rights are terminated by the agreement.

If a gay female couple uses insemination, the woman who gives birth is the sole legal parent of the child. The partner can adopt the child using a second-parent adoption procedure if it is permitted in their state. A gay male couple might use insemination coupled with egg donation and a surrogate. (See Chapter 16 for more information on egg donation; Chapter 18 for information on surrogacy.)

The *American Society of Reproductive Medicine* has a free booklet on insemination available online at: **www.asrm.org/Patients/patientbooklets/donorinsem.pdf**

Future Considerations

If you use donor insemination—whether it is from a known or unknown donor—it is important that you gather as much medical information about the donor and his family as you can find. This information will be important for your child.

Many sperm banks make it a condition of donation that the donor's identity can be revealed to children created from his sperm once they become adults. This can be an important policy that will make locating the biological parent easier for your child.

Talking about donor insemination with you child can be challenging, since it is complicated to discuss both in its physical sense as well as in an emotional sense. Be prepared for a lot of questions. Be honest with your child to the point he or she is able to understand. (See Appendix A for resources regarding books for children about insemination.)

Choosing a Sperm Bank Questionaire

Name of Agency_____

Name of Contact Person_____

Date of Interview_____

Questions:

❑ How long have you been doing this?_____
_____

❑ Are you licensed or accredited by any state or organization?___
_____

❑ Do you follow ASRM guidelines?_____
_____

❑ What procedures are used to test the health of the donors and the sperm?_____
_____

❑ What other screening do you do with donors?_____
_____

❑ How long do you keep records?_____
_____

❑ Do you follow ASRM record-keeping guidelines?_____
_____

❑ Can clients select the donor themselves?_____
_____

❑ What donor information is available?_____
_____

❑ Are current and baby pictures available from each donor?_____
_____

❑ Are personal statements available from donors?_____
_____

❑ Is the health of the donors monitored on an ongoing basis after donations are made?_____
_____

(continued)

❑ Do you track the number of pregnancies per donor? *(This is important so that there are not too many children from any one donor. Large numbers of offspring from any one donor would increase the risk that these children might someday meet and reproduce without realizing they are siblings.)*_____

_____

❑ Is donor sperm available for a second child?_____

_____

❑ Do you act as a middleman should the child, once he or she is grown, wish to contact the donor?_____

_____

❑ Is stem cell storage available from the umbilical cord?_____

_____

❑ Do you store cells from the donor that can later be tested if necessary?_____

_____

❑ Do you provide contact information so that children can contact their biological fathers?_____

_____

Chapter 16

Egg Donation

Egg donation is an option that allows a woman to carry a pregnancy, even if she does not produce eggs or produce eggs that result in pregnancy. A donor provides the eggs. The eggs are then inseminated by the woman's partner, or by a donor, and implanted in the intended mother. Some women prefer this option over adoption because not only does it allow them to have a child that is genetically related to their partner, but also because they are able to experience the pregnancy and control the environment in which the child is gestated.

Some women feel uncomfortable with the process, as if it somehow highlights their biological imperfections. Others feel uncomfortable at the notion of their husband's or partner's sperm mixing with eggs from another woman. Ultimately, using a donor is a personal choice that must be carefully considered.

Finding a Donor
Some women who need an egg donor are able to ask a family member or friend for the donation. Relatives, such as a sister or cousin, are sometimes preferred so that the child will carry similar genes as the mother.

Other women prefer to use donors who have no connection to them. These donors may be known or unknown. Some clinics have egg donor programs, where women donate eggs for compensation. Other clinics encourage women who are undergoing ART to donate extra eggs they create during the process for use by another infertile woman (often offering the donor some kind of reduced fee arrangement for her own treatment). It is also possible to locate a donor on your own, by placing ads in newspapers (particularly college newspapers) and reaching an agreement on your own with a donor.

There are a limited number of egg donors available (since the process is so arduous), and not a wide selection of donors to choose from if you are choosing a donor from those available in a clinic. If you are locating your own donor, your selection may be even smaller since few women are willing to go through the process. When you do locate an egg donor, make sure you that you obtain a complete medical history from your donor since this will be important for your child's medical care.

Search for egg donation agencies by state online at:
www.everythingsurrogacy.com/cgi-bin/main.cgi?eggagency

Donation Process

Egg donation is more complicated than sperm donation. Eggs cannot be frozen effectively yet (or, at least, it is not yet considered to be completely reliable by most specialists in this area, although technology is rapidly advancing), so the donor and the woman receiving the donation must have their cycles adjusted so that the egg can be removed from the donor and implanted into the intended mother. Both must take medication to adjust their cycles. The donor must undergo a minor surgical procedure to extract the egg, causing the risk of complications such as infection or possible damage to her ovaries.

Before the procedure, the donor is tested for various diseases. However, because the egg donation must occur immediately, eggs, unlike sperm, cannot be tested extensively.

It is highly recommended that both the donor and recipient, as well as their partners, undergo counseling to help them deal with the hormonal fluctuations of the process, as well as the emotional consequences.

Once the eggs are harvested, they are fertilized using an IVF technique or a GIFT or ZIFT technique. Fertilized eggs are implanted in the intended mother and she carries the pregnancy.

Another type of egg donation may soon be available. While it has only been successful in animals to date, it may soon be possible to transplant *ovarian tissue* (parts of the ovary) from one woman to another. This would allow an infertile recipient to create eggs using donor material. The eggs would have genetic material from the donor only, but would be grown and fertilized inside the recipient's body. Should this procedure become more common, recipients should be certain they have an agreement with the donor that any children resulting from the donation will be the intended mother's.

For more information on the donation process, see:
www.medscape.com/viewarticle/460351_2

Cost

The cost for one egg donation cycle is approximately $15,000 and includes the costs for both the donor's and recipient's care and clinic costs. If you are paying your donor additional compensation for her time or discomfort, your costs will be higher. Some donors are paid up to $7500 per cycle. Unlike in adoption or other types of donation, the donor is actually paid for her donation because it is such an arduous procedure and one that carries risks of impacting her future fertility.

Ask the clinic for a breakdown of costs for the following items:

+ application and consultation;
+ donor screening;
+ screening for you and your partner;
+ donor reimbursement;
+ drugs for donor and yourself;
+ ultrasounds and blood tests;
+ oocyte retrieval;
+ lab procedures;
+ implantation of oocytes; and,
+ freezing, storage, and thawing of oocytes.

Agreement

It is essential to use a legally binding agreement with an egg donor. It is always best to have a reproductive law attorney draw up the agreement or have your attorney check the agreement provided by the clinic. The agreement is very similar to the one used for insemination donors. Agreements state that the donor gives up all rights to the eggs and any children conceived from them. Donors have no right to custody or visitation and cannot be sued for child support. The agreement will specify that the intended parents will be financially responsible for the entire donation process, including counseling, medical costs, and prescription costs. If the donor is to be paid, the specific amount should be specified.

View a sample egg donation agreement online from the *American Surrogacy Center* at:
www.surrogacy.com/legals/eggdonationconsent.html

The donor should be required to provide a complete family medical history. Some agreements may require the donor to provide ongoing health history if conditions develop.

Both the egg donor, the recipient, and their partners (if any) should sign the agreement. The agreement should also specify that the donor (and her partner if she has one) will take any steps necessary to ensure that the child is legally that of the intended parents. Consent should also be obtained for some of the eggs to be fertilized and then frozen for future use. It important that the donor is fully informed about what is involved in the procedure and all risks that are associated with it.

State Laws

Florida, North Dakota, Oklahoma, Texas, Virginia, and Washington have laws about egg donation that state that the donor gives up her rights to the egg under a valid donation agreement, and therefore cannot be held responsible for child support and has no right to custody or visitation with any resulting children. Florida specifically allows reasonable financial compensation to the donor. Other states have no laws about egg donation.

There have been cases in both New York (*McDonald v. McDonald*) and Ohio (*Ezzone v. Ezzone*) about ownership of embryos (that have been cryopreserved) created using egg donation. In both cases, embryos were created using donor eggs and the intended father's sperm. The intended parent couples divorced and disputed ownership of the resulting embryos or custody of children born from the embryos after the divorce. In both cases, the intended mother was held to be the legal mother and the father was not given any more important rights to the embryo or child because he was biologically related to the child. (See Chapter 20 for more information about cryopreservation and disposition of eggs or embryos after divorce.)

Legal Rights

Once a donor signs a valid donor agreement, she and her spouse (if any) agree to give up all rights to any eggs donated and any children that may result from the donation. The woman who receives the donation will carry the pregnancy. The child she gives birth to is legally hers, and if she is married, her husband is the legal father.

If a single woman receives an egg donation and uses a sperm donation to fertilize the egg, she is the sole legal parent of the child.

If an unmarried couple uses egg donation and the male partner's sperm, the child is legally a child of the mother at birth. The man is not a legal father until a legally binding *paternity acknowledgment* is made (this can often be done by filing paperwork with the state putative father registry) or until a court issues a judgment of paternity. In some states (such as California) paternity can be established prior to birth if there has been adequate prebirth testing that establishes the genetic link.

It is rare for a female homosexual couple to use egg donation, since between the two women there is likely to be one partner who can ovulate without assistance. However, it is an option that is available. The partner who gives birth to the child is the legal parent and the other partner would need to use stepparent adoption to become a legal parent.

Male homosexual couples are more likely to use a surrogate who can provide the egg herself, thus making egg donation an unnecessary step.

Future Contact with the Donor

Most couples who use an unknown donor have no ongoing contact with her. More and more families that use egg donation are open about it with their children. Your donor agreement may specify that the donor is to remain anonymous or it may leave the door open for future contact. Some parents want their children to be able to locate the donor once they are adults.

Donors are usually not told if their donations result in pregnancy, so they do not have the same reactions birth mothers do in adoption situations. Most egg donors are interested in the financial incentives the program offers and are happy to know they are also able to help infertile couples. Donors are not told who gets their eggs, so they remain removed from the process.

Choosing a Clinic
Questionaire

Name of Clinic_____

Name of Contact Person_____

Date of Interview_____

Questions:

❑ Does the clinic have an existing pool of donors?_____
_____

❑ How does the clinic get donors?_____
_____

❑ How are donors compensated?_____
_____

❑ Does the clinic work with recruiters to locate donors?_____
_____

❑ What is the age range of donors?_____
_____

❑ Do donors remain anonymous?_____
_____

❑ Will you work with a donor we bring into the program?_____
_____

❑ How are donors screened?_____
_____

❑ How long is the wait to get a donor?_____
_____

❑ What amount of control do we have over the donor chosen for
us?_____
_____

❑ Are donors covered by their own or the clinic's health
insurance?_____
_____

❑ What are your statistics and success rates?_____
_____

(continued)

❏ Do you meet ASRM guidelines?_____

_____

❏ Is psychological testing done?_____

_____

❏ Will you work with our insurance company?_____

_____

❏ What payments are due at what time and what kind of refund is available if we change our minds?_____

_____

Chapter 17

Embryo Donation

Embryo donation occurs when an egg that has been fertilized and has begun to develop into a baby (sometimes also called a *zygote*—but technically an embryo is a few days older than a zygote) is donated to a mother or couple that did not provide genetic material for the child.

These embryos or zygotes are usually extras that have resulted when other couples have undergone ART procedures. Because these procedures usually produce more zygotes than are safe to implant at once, couples undergoing these procedures often freeze the extras. The original intent may be to save them for later ART cycles if the current one is unsuccessful. The couple may also intend to save them in order to have siblings later.

Although there are many ART couples producing many extra zygotes, few actually donate them to other couples. Once they have gone through the very long and difficult process of ART, these frozen embryos seem very valuable to them and it is difficult to give them away after they worked so hard to create them. Additionally, some couples may feel uncomfortable about donating them and having another couple raise their biological child. Instead, these couples often find themselves more comfortable with a zygote donated to science for research purposes only.

There have been at least fifty-three children born using embryo donation according to a recent survey by the *Embryo Donation Task Force*, and there are over 188,000 frozen embryos in America. Compared to the number of children adopted each year or conceived using other ART, this is very small. However, it is an option to consider and one that may best fit the needs of some couples.

Embryo donation is also sometimes called *embryo adoption*. The terminology used is important because it has implications for the pro-life and pro-choice movements. If it is known as embryo adoption it gives more weight to the argument that embryos are humans. Embryo donation is the term used more often since it is a more neutral term.

When you accept an embryo donation, it is like accepting a child without seeing him or her. You have no idea what you will get—and you also do not know if the embryo will actually implant. It is likely that your child will have full siblings in the world that you will never know about, since most embryo donations come from other couples undergoing ART with the purpose of having a child.

Embryo donation has been in the news recently. The federal government invested $1 million in a public awareness campaign to improve awareness about it as an option, while at the same time opposing the use of embryos for research. While this is a political power play, it has helped to bring the issue of embryo donation to the forefront.

Embryo donation has benefits and detriments. The following list looks at its pros and cons.

Embryo Donation

Pros:

+ It is much faster than adoption.
+ The intended parents completely control the pregnancy.
+ The intended mother gives birth to the baby and can nurse.
+ Genetic siblings are possible if there are enough embryos from the donor couple.
+ The process offers greater privacy than adoption.
+ Complete genetic screening is done on the embryos.
+ Complete medical information about biological parents is provided.
+ You do not have to pay an egg donor or pay for the expenses of a birth mother.
+ The legal risk is low since the donor couple never knows about the pregnancy and cannot attempt to get custody of the child or otherwise interfere.

Cons:

+ Donors tend to be people who have fertility problems themselves, so the embryos may have some problems.
+ There is very little selection or choice since there are few embryos available.
+ You cannot meet the biological parents and may not even see a photo of them.
+ Donors tend to be older.
+ Your child may have full genetic siblings in the world without your knowledge.

Finding a Donor

Some clinics arrange embryo donation and match donors and recipients themselves—with attention paid to ethnicity and physical characteristics. Recipients usually do not have the ability to select their donors as they do with other types of donation. The clinic restricts donors to those that are young enough and have no medical conditions or histories that would be of concern. Counseling is recommended for both couples in an embryo donation to make sure that everyone involved understands the process and can handle it emotionally.

You can access a list of clinics that handle embryo donation at:
www.resolve.org/main/national/embdon/ ResourceDirectory.pdf

Embryo Adoption

Another option is an embryo adoption, which is a modified form of embryo donation and is not to be confused with the term of the same name sometimes used for embryo donation. (see p.185.) An outside agency that is not associated with the clinic handles the matching process. Recipients are provided with more information about the donors and counseling and home studies are performed in much the same way they would be in a traditional adoption. Donors have some say in choosing the recipient and also have the option of staying in touch with them and possibly knowing their genetic children at some point down the line.

Snowflakes is one of the only agencies that handles embryo adoptions in a process similar to traditional adoptions. They can be contacted at:

Snowflakes
Nightlight Christian Adoptions
801 East Chapman, Suite 106
Fullerton, CA 92831
714-278-1020
www.snowflakes.org

For embryo donation information you can contact *Reprotech* at:
www.reprot.com

National Embryo Donation Center at:
www.embryodonation.org

State Laws

California, Florida, Louisiana, North Dakota, Oklahoma, and Texas have laws permitting embryo donation that make the recipient or recipient couple the legal parent or parents. Florida permits reasonable compensation to the donors. Other states do not have laws about embryo adoption or donation. The process is handled by the contract created by the parties.

The recipient mother or couple is/are the legal parent(s) of a child born through embryo donation or adoption. As soon as the embryo is implanted in the mother, she is its legal parent because under state laws, the woman who gives birth to the baby is its legal mother. Her husband is the legal father, since under state law the husband of a woman who has a baby is its legal father. If she has an unmarried partner he can adopt the child via second parent adoption. This same procedure applies to gay female couples.

Some couples that accept donations are not comfortable with the lack of law in this area and thus seek to protect themselves by going through an adoption procedure after the child is born, since if DNA tests were ever done, it would prove the child to be the product of the biological donors. It is important to talk to your reproductive rights attorney about how you can best protect your family and follow your state's laws.

> Information about embryo adoption is available through *RESOLVE* (the National Infertility Association) at:
> **www.resolve.org/main/national/embdon/index.jsp**

Costs

Costs for embryo donation are similar to those for IVF, but there may be additional costs for the donation of the embryo. Costs average $3000 per transfer. If your embryo is being shipped to you, you will have additional shipping costs, which run in the hundreds since the embryo must be carefully preserved during the shipping process. The donor couple is not paid for the donation.

Agreement

Generally, there are two separate agreements involved in embryo donation. The donors sign an agreement giving up all rights to the frozen embryos. This could occur years before a recipient is found. Often, this is part of the original contract that the couple signs when they begin ART at the clinic. Most agreements specify what will happen to unused or extra embryos. The recipients sign a separate agreement with the clinic agreeing to accept the embryo and dealing with the medical risk factors involved. Recipients must receive full disclosure of all risks. Donors and recipients usually have no direct contact and are not aware of each other's identity. Be sure to have your reproductive law attorney read any contract from a clinic before you sign it.

The agreement should contain the following:
+ a complete release of all rights by the donors;
+ a clear explanation of costs;
+ a description of what happens if an embryo does not thaw and cannot be implanted;
+ an indication that you have received full disclosure and understand the risks involved;
+ an agreement as to whether or not you will receive additional donations should they be needed; and,
+ a treatment program you will be receiving.

If you are interested in an embryo donation in which the donors are involved in the selection process, you will find that there are no laws governing this process. Agencies that take this approach treat the process as a traditional adoption and have the donor and recipient sign consent forms as they would in a regular adoption.

A sample agreement for embryo donation can be read at:
**www.dreamababy.com/download_files/
Embryo%20Donation%20Stipulation%20Agreement.pdf**

Issues

There are a lot of issues involved with this type of donation. First is the consideration that if you are trying to conceive, you may not get the best possible results by using an embryo created by another couple that was having trouble conceiving themselves.

Because a number of embryos usually must be implanted in order to achieve one viable pregnancy, couples are faced with the problem of trying to find a donor that can provide more than one embryo or opt to use embryos from several donors simultaneously. Should twins result, they could have completely different genetic parents. Also, the parents would never know which donor couple created the child and could spend an inordinate amount of time looking for characteristics or hints from the children themselves.

Privacy

Another issue involved with embryo donation is privacy. It is possible to keep the fact of the donation to yourselves and not share the information with family and friends. Some people choose not to share this information because they believe their child would be treated differently or that their family and friends would have a negative reaction to the donation. Some family members are unable to let the information go and spend years wondering aloud about the donors and their characteristics. It is, however, important to share the donation with your obstetrician and pediatrician in case there is ever a health issue that could be impacted by the donation fact.

Some parents decide to share information about the donation with their child, while others prefer not to reveal this information. As with adoption, it is a matter of personal preference how much you want to share with your child and what you feel comfortable revealing.

Clinic Evaluation Questionaire

Name of Clinic_____

Name of Contact Person_____

Date of Interview_____

Questions:

❏ What kind of release have the donors signed?_____

_____

❏ Do they relinquish all rights to the embryos?_____

_____

❏ How many embryos are available from this couple?_____

_____

❏ Do you ever recommend using a mixture of embryos from different couples?_____

_____

❏ Will I learn the names of the donors?_____

_____

❏ Will the donors learn our names?_____

_____

❏ What information can I learn about the donors?_____

_____

❏ What medical and family history is available?_____

_____

❏ Are photographs of the donor couple available? (*Some recipients like to have photos to show their children or to get a sense of what their baby might look like.*)_____

_____

❏ How do you match donors and recipients?_____

_____

❏ Do we have any say in how the clinic matches donors and recipients?_____

_____

(continued)

❑ Does the donor couple have a say in how the clinic matches donors and recipients?_____

_____

❑ What is your success rate with embryo donation?_____

_____

❑ How many embryo donation transfers have you performed?___

_____

❑ How long have you been performing this procedure?_____

_____

❑ Have any children resulted from embryos from this couple? (*You will want to know if your child has any living siblings.*)_____

_____

❑ Have embryos from this couple been donated to anyone else and will they be in the future? (*You want to be sure that no one else is receiving donations to limit the number of siblings out there in the world for your child.*)_____

_____

❑ What was the age of the donors at the time of donation? (*Younger is better.*)_____

_____

❑ How long has the embryo been frozen? (*An older embryo may not be as effective as a newer one.*)_____

_____

❑ What kind of treatment did the donating couple undergo?____

_____

❑ Why did they donate the embryos?_____

_____

❑ Are the eggs and sperm used to create the embryo the donor couple's own or were they donations?_____

_____

❑ If the eggs and sperm used to create the embryo were donations, what information is available about these donors?_____

_____

(continued)

❏ What screening and testing has been done of the donor couple and the donated embryos?_____

❏ If the embryos do not survive thawing, what financial adjustments or refunds are made? (*You want some kind of adjustment.*)___

❏ What are the total fees for this process?_____

❏ What support services are available?_____

Chapter 18

Surrogacy

Surrogacy is perhaps the most controversial of all ARTs currently available. A surrogate is a woman who agrees to carry a pregnancy for another person or couple. There are two types of surrogacy—one where the surrogate is biologically related to the child and the other where she has no biological connection. In *traditional surrogacy*, the surrogate's own eggs are used and are inseminated with the intended father's sperm. *Gestational surrogacy* occurs when the surrogate is implanted with an embryo created with the intended parents' genetic material or with donor eggs or sperm.

Surrogacy can cost from $25,000 to over $50,000, depending on the difficulty involved with conception, the medical issues present in the pregnancy, and what expenses and costs the intended parents are responsible for under the contract.

Laws Concerning Surrogacy

There is no general legal trend about surrogacy in the United States yet, and states tend to be all over the board. As such, five general categories of how states address surrogacy have developed.

States where it is a crime to pay for surrogacy:
- Michigan
- New Mexico

- New York
- Utah
- Washington

Areas where surrogacy contracts are *unenforceable:* (This means you cannot ask a court to enforce it, however you are free to enter into one, knowing you will not be able to obtain assistance from the court):

- District of Columbia
- Indiana
- Louisiana
- Nebraska
- New York (you are free to enter into an unpaid agreement, but it is a crime to pay for surrogacy)
- North Dakota
- Virginia

States that *recognize* surrogacy agreements through laws:

- Arkansas
- Florida (reasonable compensation is permitted)
- New Hampshire
- Nevada
- Tennessee
- Texas
- Washington (you cannot pay for surrogacy, but you can agree to unpaid surrogacy)
- West Virginia

States that have *caselaw* about surrogacy:

- California (permits surrogacy)
- Kentucky (prohibits surrogacy programs and payments, but this is largely unenforced)

✦ Massachusetts (a recent case encouraged the legislature to enact laws permitting surrogacy)

✦ Ohio (surrogate who is biologically related must relinquish rights in order for intended mother to become legal parent and the state will not enforce surrogacy contracts)

✦ Oklahoma (permits surrogacy, but requires the surrogate's husband (if any) to refuse to consent to what is technically considered to be an egg donation to the surrogate—in other words, even if the surrogate is using her own eggs, the law acts as if eggs were donated to her and her husband then does not consent to the donation, so his rights are eliminated)

(All other states do not specifically address surrogacy.)

Surrogacy is an emotional issue for many people, which is why the states do not agree. Some people vehemently oppose it, suggesting it is like selling a baby or renting a womb. Other people feel it is a logical extension of adoption and is an option that presents couples with a greater opportunity to bond with the baby and include the birth mother in the child's life.

The Legal Process of Surrogacy

In states that do not have laws stating otherwise, when a woman gives birth to a child, she is the legal mother of the child, even if she is not the biological mother of the child or has entered into a surrogacy contract. If the woman is married, her husband is considered to be the child's legal father.

When a surrogacy agreement is entered into, the surrogate's husband must be a party to the contract and must revoke his rights to the child. If the intended father is the biological father, he can obtain an *order of paternity* (in some states this can happen during the pregnancy). This gives him the legal right to have access to the child at the hospital and to take the child home without any additional legal steps. The next step that must happen is that the intended mother must adopt the child in a second-parent adoption procedure. (See Chapter 4 for more information.) A few states that do not require stepparent adoption by the intended mother include Arkansas, Florida, and West Virginia (adoption is not required if the intended parents provided the embryo).

California Procedure

California is one of the few states that has a fairly well-established procedure for legalizing a surrogate birth. The intended parents file a court case during the pregnancy. The surrogate and her husband consent to the surrogacy in the case. The court issues a judgment that the intended parents are the legal parents. The intended parents then can inform the hospital of this and the birth certificate will be issued to them. They have the right to select the child's name.

However, if the surrogate provides the egg, she cannot relinquish her rights until the child is born (as in an adoption proceeding). In this case, the intended father can bring a paternity case during the pregnancy. Then the surrogate and her husband consent and the intended father is the legal father. The intended mother must use the second-parent adoption procedure to legalize her role.

Surrogacy Programs

Many couples locate a surrogate through a surrogacy program managed through a fertility clinic. Adoption agencies also often coordinate surrogacy programs. These programs locate potential surrogates, prescreen them, and match them with parents.

The ideal surrogate is married and has children of her own—this is because she is presumed to be mature and in a stable relationship. Being married means she has support from her husband and also has someone to financially support her during pregnancy. It also means that, presumably, most of her emotional needs are being met and she will not look to the baby to fulfill them. Having children is important because it means she understands what it is like to be pregnant and give birth. It is supposedly easier for her to carry this child for someone else and walk away if she has a real understanding of what pregnancy and birth are like and really knows the kinds of emotions she may feel after giving birth.

A woman who has never had children may be surprised at how strongly she feels about the baby when it is born and may be unable to give it up. The thinking is that a surrogate who is a parent has been through it all and enters the agreement with experience. This does not mean that a married surrogate with children of her own will not change her mind—but it does tend to improve the odds. Adoption agencies that have surrogacy programs treat the entire process in the same way they would a regular adoption and require home studies, counseling, and communication between the parties.

It is important to choose a surrogacy program that you feel comfortable with and confident in. Once you find a potential surrogate, it is necessary that she undergo physical and mental exams before any contract is entered into. The surrogate will also want to get to know you and decide if she feels comfortable with you. You, of course, will do the same with her. Since surrogacy involves a large degree of trust, it is important to use a surrogate you are completely comfortable with.

Finding a Surrogate on Your Own

Another option for surrogacy is to locate a surrogate on your own, without using a program. A sister, relative, or close friend may be willing to be a surrogate. Of course, in this situation, it is essential to use a reproductive law attorney who will advise you as to the laws in your state and will draw up a contract. Additionally, it is important that everyone involved in the surrogacy process obtain counseling, since this emotional situation is further compounded by the existing relationships. It is possible to locate a stranger surrogate on your own, but this is not recommended since you cannot perform the same sophisticated screening and psychological evaluation an agency or clinic can.

Surrogacy Agreements

Surrogacy agreements are complicated and important documents. The most important feature of a surrogacy agreement is that it revokes all rights and responsibilities the surrogate and her husband have to the child. The intended parents are the legal parents to the child. Other important clauses include:

- ✦ the surrogate agrees to follow all medical advice, but medical decisions during the pregnancy are ultimately left up to her;
- ✦ the surrogate agrees to consider selective reduction if necessary;
- ✦ the state where the child will be born is specified;
- ✦ the intended parents take on all financial and medical responsibility for the child;
- ✦ the intended parents have the right to name the child;
- ✦ the surrogate agrees to use her own medical insurance if she has any to cover her care during the pregnancy and delivery; and,
- ✦ the surrogate agrees to abstain from intercourse for a period of time while conception is attempted.

Read a sample surrogacy contract at:
www.surrogacy.com/legals/gestcontract.html
www.surromomsonline.com/articles/contract.htm
www.everythingsurrogacy.com/cgi-bin/main.cgi?test

It is essential that you use an attorney experienced in surrogacy agreements. Even if you are working with an agency or surrogacy program, you should hire your own attorney to review the contract.

Some people may wonder why an agreement is so essential, particularly if they live in a state where the courts will not uphold a surrogacy agreement. Even if your courts will not enforce a surrogacy agreement, it would still be important evidence should you get into a custody battle with your surrogate. Agreements are also important because the negotiation process can help you spot and work out things that might be potential problems down the line. The agreement will spell out in clear terms what everyone is going to do and how all the issues involved will be handled. Also, when people sign their name to a contract, they will usually feel obligated to carry out what they are agreeing to, so the agreement is an important way for both you and the surrogate to commit to the surrogacy.

Payment Issues

The issue of paying surrogates is probably the most controversial part of the entire surrogacy process. Some people argue that paying a surrogate amounts to buying a baby and should be outlawed. Others feel that surrogates should be compensated for their time, physical discomfort, emotional turmoil, and extreme generosity.

The intended parents will always take on all medical expenses relating to the conception, pregnancy, and birth. In many cases, you will also be permitted to reimburse the surrogate for travel expenses, maternity clothes, loss of wages, and additional child care expenses. The laws governing this are the same as the laws governing reimbursement of expenses for a birth mother in an adoption. (See Chapter 8 for more information.) Payment is often made through your attorney so there is a clear record that can be presented to the court as proof that all is done in a very forthright and honest manner.

Some states do permit payments to the surrogate to compensate her for time and discomfort. While payments are not permitted in other states, it is possible to give the surrogate a gift. Discuss this option with your attorney to find out what is permissible in your state. There may be rules about the value of the gift—it must really be a gift, not a form of payment. Some parents give their surrogate a special piece of jewelry or something else that has sentimental value and meaning. If you violate the law about payments, your parent-child relationship is not jeopardized, however, you may be subject to criminal penalties.

Insurance Coverage

If your surrogate has insurance coverage, it should cover her pregnancy. Some surrogates do not wish to use their own insurance. Others are willing to do so, if the intended parents pay all deductibles and co-pays. This is an important part of your agreement and should be included in your contract.

If your surrogate does not have health insurance coverage or will not be using her own coverage, you will need to pay for her medical expenses yourself or help her obtain a health insurance policy (which may mean paying for it yourself). Your insurance will not provide coverage until the birth, and then only if one parent is already a legal parent or if the child is officially placed with you as part of the adoption process.

Problems with Surrogacy

Many people are leery of surrogacy agreements, having heard about high profile cases in which surrogates changed their minds and refused to place the child with the intended parents. In some ways, the prospect of this is scarier than that of an adoption in which the birth mother changes her mind, since in most cases, the intended father is also the biological and legal father of the baby.

Perhaps the most famous case about surrogacy is the *Baby M* case from New Jersey in 1988. In that case, the court invalidated the surrogacy agreement, but placed the baby with the biological father. The intended mother was not permitted to adopt since the surrogate (who was the biological mother) did not give her consent. The court found that the surrogacy agreement was invalid because the surrogate was paid. If the agreement did not include payment, it would have been valid.

Another landmark case is the *Johnson v. Calvert* case decided in California in 1993. In this case, the surrogate was implanted with a zygote that was created using genetic material from both the intended mother and intended father. The surrogate was not biologically related to the child. The court held that the legal parents are those who were intended to be the parents under the agreement. According to the court, the parent of a surrogate child is whoever is intended by the parties to be the parent, not who is biologically related to the child or who carries the pregnancy.

An Ohio case, *Belsito v. Clark*, from 1994, held that unless legal waiver or consent is provided, the people who provide the genetic material for the child are the natural parents of the child. This means that if the surrogate provides the egg, she is the legal mother, but can give her consent for the adoption.

In most cases, a surrogate does not change her mind, especially when you use a respected surrogacy program that will carefully screen all potential surrogates and help you find a good match. However, should something go wrong and the surrogate changes her mind, you first need to consult an attorney so that you can fully understand the laws in your state. As described earlier in this chapter, some states will not enforce surrogacy contracts.

If the intended father is the biological father of the child, at the very minimum, he will have access to the child until the case is resolved. There is a very good chance that the father will be able to obtain custody, and through him, the intended mother would be able to have time with the child. If the surrogate provided the egg, she will at the very least be entitled to have contact with the child (unless the birth is in a state where surrogacy contracts are enforced). If the surrogate did not provide the egg, the case for the intended parents is stronger, but not completely decided unless your state enforces surrogacy agreements.

Note: *Some people go to California to enter into surrogacy contracts since the laws there are the clearest and have a definite legal procedure in place.*

The surrogate's husband would have an initial claim to the child, since any child born to a woman during marriage is legally considered to be her husband's legal child. However, DNA tests would make it clear who the real father is and the husband's claim would be denied.

If a surrogate is related to the child and she changes her mind, and your state does not uphold agreements, you are facing a situation where the child would have to split his or her time between you and the surrogate. It is for this reason that many people are particular about the states in which they enter into surrogacy agreements.

Other Steps to Protect Yourself

As soon as you have entered into a surrogacy agreement, it is essential that you have a will drawn up or update an existing will. You will want to name a *guardian* for your child should anything happen to you. You want to have a clear legal plan for who would care for your child should you and your spouse pass away.

If you must go through a second-parent adoption process to make the intended mother the legal mother, there will likely be weeks or months until the adoption is final. In this time period, the father will have all the legal rights to make medical decisions for the child, but the intended mother will only have these rights if they are given to her in writing. The father should execute a written consent giving the mother the right to make medical decisions for the child.

Choosing a Surrogacy Program Questionaire

Name of Agency_____

Name of Contact Person_____

Date of Interview_____

Questions:

❑ How do you recruit and locate surrogates?_____
_____

❑ How do you screen potential surrogates?_____
_____

❑ How do you screen the intended parents?_____
_____

❑ Do you provide counseling for both surrogate and intended
parents?_____
_____

❑ What is your role in coordinating the surrogacy?_____
_____

❑ What fees are involved?_____
_____

❑ Are the fees refundable if the surrogacy is not completed?_____
_____

❑ Does this differ with miscarriage as opposed to a surrogate
who changes her mind?_____
_____

❑ Is there a waiting list?_____
_____

❑ How many potential surrogates do you have in the program?____
_____

❑ How many intended parents are you working with now?_____
_____

❑ Will you work with surrogates brought in by the intended
parents?_____
_____

(continued)

❑ What kind of relationship do you recommend that intended parents have with their surrogate?_____

_____

❑ Is there any post-birth contact with your program?_____

_____

❑ Have any of your surrogates changed their minds after becoming pregnant?_____

_____

❑ How do you handle this situation?_____

_____

❑ How many births does your program have a year?_____

_____

❑ How many total births have you had?_____

_____

❑ How long have you been doing this?_____

_____

❑ Can you provide the names of parents to contact for references?

_____

❑ Do intended parents have the right to refuse proposed surrogates?_____

_____

❑ Does the surrogate have her own attorney when signing the agreement?_____

_____

❑ What kind of background information do you provide about the surrogate?_____

_____

❑ How do you deal with the surrogate's expenses?_____

_____

❑ How are they accounted and paid for?_____

_____

Chapter 19

Emerging Technologies

The technology of ART is always advancing and changing. There are new treatments and options on the horizon that may someday be widely available.

Nuclear Transfer

Nuclear transfer is a process in which the *nucleus* of an egg cell, the part that contains the genetic material, is removed and replaced with another nucleus. This procedure could be used by women who are unable to produce viable egg cells on their own. The intended mother's genetic material would be implanted into an egg donated by another woman. The egg would then carry the intended mother's genes, but would also contain *mitochrondrial genes* from the donor. These genes do not determine physical traits but can carry inherited diseases, so the resulting child would be influenced by the donor but would be directly related to the intended mother. This newly formed egg could then be inseminated and placed in the intended mother's uterus or in that of a surrogate. The procedure has been attempted with human eggs, but there have been no reported positive results at the time this book was written.

Another option with this technique would be to replace the nucleus of the donor egg with the nucleus from a sperm. The newly created egg would then be fertilized by a different sperm. A child born by this technique would have two genetic parents who are both male. Although this has not been attempted yet, it is something that would be of great interest to the gay community.

If this procedure ever does become available, it will be important to obtain complete consent of all the parties involved, including the woman who provides the donor egg. A complete medical history will be essential since the donor egg can carry disease. Additionally, it will be important that the contract completely revokes the donor's rights and responsibilities towards the egg and any resulting child. This procedure is currently banned in California under its human cloning law.

In Vitro Maturation

Instead of stimulating women's ovaries to produce mature eggs, this technique allows eggs to be matured in vitro in the laboratory. This technique can be used by women who will be using their own eggs, as well as donor eggs. Legal issues may include storage, record keeping, and donor issues with any donated material.

For more information on in vitro maturation, see:
www.infertilitytutorials.com/procedures_members/invitro.cfm

Cytoplasmic Transfer

Some women produce eggs that have defective *cytoplasm*, the material that fills the egg and gives it energy. This technique removes cytoplasm from a donor egg and injects it into the mother's egg. At least one child has been born using this technique.

As with other egg donation procedures, it is important to obtain the consent of all the parties involved and to have a contract that completely removes the donor's rights and responsibilities towards the egg, cytoplasm, and any child that is created from it.

For more information on cytoplasmic transfer, go to:
www.inciid.org/cytoplasmic%2Dtransfer.html

Cloning

Cloning is the most controversial area of ART and has received a lot of media coverage in the past few years. The type of cloning used in reproduction is called *somatic nuclear cloning* and is the same type that was used to create *Dolly* the sheep.

There are numerous applications of cloning that are useful in ART and too often they are obscured by the emotional reaction people have to the word *cloning*. Most people think of cloning as the process by which an exact replica of a specific human is created. With that technique, the nucleus of an embryo is removed and is replaced with DNA from an adult. It is then implanted. The result is an exact genetic twin to the person who donated the DNA.

Other applications may prove more useful and less controversial. Both sperm and eggs can be cloned, so a couple seeking ART could go through just one ART egg harvesting cycle, clone the harvested eggs, and then have innumerable eggs available for future fertilization. This would avoid the need to go through *superovulation* and the discomfort of the egg harvesting procedure again. Additionally, if a man has a low sperm count, his sperm could be cloned, making it possible to attempt many more insemination procedures.

Another type of cloning is *embryo cloning*. An infertile couple could create just one successfully fertilized embryo and clone it so numerous attempts at implantation could be made.

It should also be noted that there are other types of cloning used by medical science that do not involve the reproduction of humans. These other types of cloning are used to find cures for various diseases and for scientific research. They do not involve the creation of an identical human being or even a human embryo.

Clonaid, a human cloning company, has reported the birth of five babies through the use of cloning. For more information about this company, see:

www.clonaid.com

or

The Human Clone Rights Foundation at:

www.humanclonerights.org

Legal Prevention

There has been much talk about passing laws to prevent cloning. Currently only a few states have created legislation banning reproductive cloning: Arkansas; California; Iowa; Michigan; North Dakota; Rhode Island; and Virginia. Louisiana had a law prohibiting reproductive cloning, but at the time this book was printed, the law had expired and had not yet been renewed.

Choosing Cloning

While reproductive cloning is not readily available, it is an option that may become more viable in the future. Should you ever consider cloning, it will be important to distinguish between the types of reproductive cloning being offered to you. Since little data is available about the long-term effect of human reproductive cloning, it will be a good idea to review the results of studies that have been conducted and to evaluate all long-term data available. Additionally, it will be important to ensure that the laboratory and facilities performing the procedure are experienced and have had past successes with the treatment being sought—the number of take home babies per procedures performed.

Carefully read all contracts and have them closely reviewed by a reproductive law attorney before signing anything. It will be important to understand what procedures are in place to label and identify genetic material that is being stored and worked on; what medical procedures will be used to create the pregnancy; and, all the costs and fees involved in the procedure.

Many people have moral and religious views about cloning as a reproductive choice, thus it is important to completely understand what genetic material is being duplicated; what the resulting child will be like; and, how all of these facts impact the parents.

LEGAL RAMIFICATIONS OF CLONING

There are few legal ramifications to cloning egg or sperm cells, if they are for one's own use. If cells such as these are cloned and then donated, the issues involved are similar to those for other sperm or egg donations, except children resulting from multiple cloned eggs or sperms would be more genetically similar than is usual in egg or sperm donation situations.

Embryo cloning creates embryos that are identical multiples. Couples using this technology might have identical twins born at the same time or could have one child and later have another child from a cloned embryo, creating genetic twins that are born years apart. Although identical twins have the same DNA, there are differences between them that stem from their environment. Children created using this method would have identical DNA and thus could not be distinguished using DNA tests. Other identifying features (such as scars or growth differences) can be used to distinguish them, should it ever be necessary. Modern fingerprinting is also able to discern the difference between identical twins most of the time.

Somatic nuclear cloning of an adult raises legal issues similar to that of embryo cloning. The child that is born would have DNA identical to the parent's, making him or her an identical twin to the parent. However, as with embryo cloning, environment would have an impact on the child and thus, he or she could not be exactly the same as the parent and it would be possible to distinguish between them.

Chapter 20

Cryopreservation

Cryopreservation, the subzero freezing of human cells, has opened many doors and provided a lot of flexibility for ART. Cryopreservation is used to freeze sperm, eggs (although this application is not completely foolproof yet), and embryos and save them for future use by the person or couple who created them or save them for donation to other infertile singles or couples. Cryopreservation is an important option for those facing chemotherapy, which can permanently damage sperm and egg production capabilities, or for women who are approaching menopause and may not be able to produce viable eggs in the future. Couples undergoing ART often choose to cryopreserve sperm, eggs, or embryos for later use. It is also possible to preserve eggs or sperm for use after your death.

Contract

The cryopreservation agreement is usually part of your overall contract with the clinic when you choose to undergo ART. When you choose to cryopreserve your reproductive material, make sure your contract addresses:

+ cost;
+ ownership (and addresses issues such as death or divorce);
+ length of preservation;

+ disposal or donation preferences;
+ cryopreservation technique;
+ steps that have been taken by the facility to protect the frozen material in a disaster, such as loss of power;
+ what will happen if the facility closes (whether you will be given notice and time to transfer your material to another facility); and,
+ the success rate with material that has been cryopreserved at that facility.

When you receive donated sperm, eggs, or embryos, you may have the option of cryopreserving the material you do not use immediately. Should you choose to do so, make sure your contract includes the items mentioned above, as well as:

+ relinquishment of rights by donor(s);
+ agreement that the genetic material can be used or frozen for future use;
+ disclosure of genetic risk factors and family medical history by the donor;
+ waiver of any right to collect child support against the donor(s); and,
+ identification of recipient(s) as legal parent(s).

Cost
There is usually an up-front fee for cryopreservation (up to $1000) and then a monthly storage fee. Any fees for IVF, insemination, or embryo transfer would be completely separate and not included in this fee.

Divorce
There have been several high profile cases about disputes among divorced couples about how their cryopreserved eggs, sperm, and embryos are to be used.

In New Jersey, in *J.B. v. M.B.* (June 2000), the court determined that frozen embryos from the marriage could be destroyed even though only one party agreed. In New York, *Maureen Kass v. Stephen Kass* (May 1998) held that even though the ex-wife wanted to implant the embryos, the embryos should be donated for research as the couple had agreed at the time they entered treatment.

There is a general consensus emerging among courts that there is a right *not* to be a parent. The position is that taking someone's genetic material and using it to create a child they do not want is almost a kind of rape and a violation of basic human rights. The issue is inflammatory because it again comes down to basic differences about how embryos should be treated and what legal status they should be given. Many clinics now include a clause in the contract stating that both the husband and wife must consent to the use, donation, or destruction of cryopreserved embryos.

Some states are beginning to address this situation. For example, in Florida, a written agreement is required that deals with what will happen with the eggs, sperm, or embryos in the event of a divorce.

It is a very good idea to designate in your cryopreservation agreement exactly what is to happen to the embryos in the event of divorce or death of one or both partners. The *Kass* decision in New York stated that the court should always look to the original agreement and try to uphold it no matter what changes happen in the meantime. This means that when you are making these decisions, you should carefully think through the various scenarios that could confront you in the future and how you would want the embryos to be handled in those situations.

Death of a Parent

Another troublesome issue has been the use of cryopreserved eggs, sperm, or embryos after the death of one of the intended parents. Some parents have had difficulty having their child legally recognized as the child of the pre-deceased parent. Some states have stepped in to legislate this issue with all of the following recognizing the deceased's parentage:

+ Colorado
+ Florida
+ Louisiana
+ North Dakota
+ Texas
+ Virginia
+ Washington
+ Wyoming

A Massachusetts case, *Woodward v. Commissioner of Social Security* (January 2002), held that children born to a parent after his or her death can inherit from him or her under the state's inheritance laws.

If you have cryopreserved material or if you plan to cryopreserve material, it is important to include information about it in your will. It is possible to pass ownership of this material to your spouse, your children, or anyone else you choose. It is important to think about these issues now and decide how you would want the genetic material handled so that you can be sure your wishes will be carried out.

Chapter 21

Raising an ART Child

Raising a child conceived with ART is like raising any other child, except you have some additional challenges. You must decide how and when you will explain your child's conception to him or her. You also must deal with reactions from others who learn of the path you took. Additionally, you will have to make choices about what, if any, contact your child will have now or in the future with donors or surrogates and deal with any possible health consequences your child will face.

Explaining Things to Your Child

Some parents never tell their child that they used ART to achieve conception, while others feel an obligation to explain this to the child. The path you take is your choice. Parents who use ART, but do so without a donor or surrogate, may feel there is no need to explain the complicated procedures to a child and may save the explanation for when the child is older.

If you do feel that you want to be open with your child, there are a number of things to consider.

+ Do you want to share all the information you have about a donor or surrogate with your child?

+ Do you want to paint this person in the same way you might a biological parent who placed a child for adoption?

✦ Is this donor or surrogate in more of a helper role in your mind?

Whatever explanation you choose can be challenging. Remember to only tell your child what he or she can handle at his or her current age. There are details children are not able to understand. Break it down into easy-to-understand explanations.

See Appendix A for additional books about assisted reproduction. Some books about assisted reproduction are available at:
www.donor-conception-network.org/basechildbooks.htm

Coping with Other People

While your close friends and family may be aware of your use of ART, they may not completely understand how you want to approach the topic and deal with it as you raise your child. If possible, it is best to set basic ground rules. You might want to be the only person who discusses this topic with your child, and may ask others not to mention it. If you have no plans to tell your child, then you will need to be sure friends and family can keep a secret. If you have a specific approach you want to take in explaining the ART circumstances to your child, be sure to tell your family and friends how you are going to approach this.

As your child grows, there will be other circumstances when the information about his or her conception will become relevant. Your pediatrician will need to know all the information about the conception of your child and the medical history of donors or surrogates may become important at some point should your child develop certain illnesses or conditions. Your child may bring up his or her conception at school or with friends and you may be required to step in and give more accurate explanations.

You may have various uncomfortable encounters where people will assume your child is genetically related to you or your spouse, when in fact he or she is not. Some parents choose to ignore these comments or gloss over them since they feel no need to explain their family's intimate details. Other parents feel a need to set the record straight.

If you are a single parent or a gay couple, people may ask uncomfortable questions about your child's biological parentage. Again, different parents have different reactions to these comments. You will have to find the path with which you are most comfortable.

Medical Information

If you use a donor or surrogate, you will receive medical history information. It will be important to save this information for your child. If the clinic or sperm bank you work with updates donors' medical information, ask if you will automatically receive updates when they are available or if you will have to contact the clinic or bank to obtain updated information.

Helping Your Child Locate
His or Her Donors or Surrogates

When your child is a teen or an adult, he or she may wish to find and meet the donor or surrogate who participated in his or her conception. Some sperm banks will receive requests from children and forward them to donors, while others will not. If this opportunity is something you want to make available to your child, make sure to ask the bank's policy about this before selecting a donor. Some egg donor clinics are willing to pass along requests from children as well, but since egg donors are less common than sperm donors, this does not happen as frequently. There is generally no contact information available about embryo donation, unless it is handled similar to an open adoption.

Other sperm banks allow children or parents to make contact with other families that used the same donor's sperm, allowing the children to meet and have relationships with their half-siblings.

ART children and parents can try to locate donors using donor registries, such as this one: **www.abolishadoption.com/DonorOffspring.html**

Parents can try to locate their children's half-siblings through registries, such as this one: **http://mattes.home.pipeline.com/sibling.html**

Epilogue

This book has presented you with a wide variety of choices and options for building a family. You may feel more comfortable with some options than with others. You may also start down one path and later decide to follow another. There are no right or wrong choices—there are only those that work for you. As you face new decisions or challenges, this book can help you work through the choices and problems you face.

My hope is that this book helps you find the child of your heart.

Glossary

A

adoptee. Person being adopted.

adoption. A process whereby a child becomes part of another's family through legal means.

adult adoption. Adoption by one adult of another adult.

B

birth father. The biological father of the child.

birth mother. The biological mother of the child. Also sometimes defined as the woman who physically gave birth to the child.

birth parent. The biological parent of the child.

blastocyst. An early embryo.

C

closed adoption. An adoption whereby the child has no information about the birth parents.

consent. A legal agreement that an adoption should take place.

consulate. A government's office in another country, through which it can assist citizens visiting the foreign country.

cryopreservation. The freezing of eggs, sperm, or embryos.

D

domestic adoption. An adoption of a child born in the United States.

donor. A person who donates egg, sperm, or embryo for another to use.

E

embassy. An official headquarters of a government inside a foreign country.

embryo. An egg fertilized with sperm that has begun to divide.

embryo adoption. A process in which an embryo is donated to another couple or person and adoption-type procedures are followed, such as home studies and possible contact between the parties.

embryo donation. A donation to another couple or for use in research of an embryo created during ART.

F

facilitator. A professional who arranges adoptions.

foster care. A situation in which a child that is in the custody of the state is temporarily cared for by adults licensed by the state.

G

gamete. An egg or sperm cell.

gamete intrafallopian transfer (GIFT). A technique in which eggs are placed into the intended mother's fallopian tubes with large numbers of sperm.

guardianship. A legal proceeding giving someone the authority to make decisions for another person, usually a child or a person who is mentally incompetent.

H

home study. A process through which a licensed social worker meets with prospective adoptive parents and evaluates their lifestyle and home for its appropriateness to house a child.

intra cytoplasmic sperm injection (ICSI). An injection into an egg of a single sperm, also called *microinsemination.*

I

Immigration and Naturalization Service (INS). The previous name of the department whose duties are now administered by the USCIS.

independent adoption. An adoption in which the adoptive parent locates the child or birth mother instead of having an agency do so.

Indian Child Welfare Act. A federal law specifying that a Native American child must be placed with relatives, within the tribe, or with other Native Americans before other options are considered.

insemination. A process of inserting sperm into a woman's body or into eggs in a laboratory to achieve conception.

international adoption. An adoption of a child born in another country.

in vitro fertilization (IVF). When an egg is fertilized with sperm in a laboratory.

intrauterine insemination (IVI). A superovualtion is induced and a large number of sperm is inserted into the uterus.

K
kinship adoption. An adoption of a child that is a relative.

kinship agreement. An agreement outlining contact that birth parents and other relatives will have with a child that has been adopted.

L
legal risk placement. A placement of a foster care child who may need to be reunited with his or her parents.

M

minor. A child under the age of eighteen.

mitrochondrial genes. Specific genes that do not determine physical traits, but can carry inherited diseases.

N

notice. A legal notification of an adoption proceeding.

O

oocyte. An egg cell.

open adoption. An adoption in which the child is aware that he or she was adopted and one in which he or she may or may not have contact with the birth parents.

P

parent-initiated adoption. An adoption in which the adoptive parent locates the child or birth mother instead of having an agency do so.

petition. A legal document asking a court to approve an adoption.

R

revocation. Legally taking back your consent for an adoption.

S

second-parent adoption. An adoption of a child by his or her stepparent.

social worker. A professional who performs home studies and assists families with adjustments to adoptions.

somatic nuclear cloning. Replacing the nucleus of a cell with a cell from another person.

special needs child. A child that has a physical or mental disability.

surrogacy. The process by which a surrogate carries a pregnancy for the intended parent(s) and has no legal ties to the child.

surrogate. A woman who carried a pregnancy for the intended parent(s) without any legal ties to the child.

U
United States Citizenship and Immigration Services (USCIS). A division of the Department of Homeland Security.

V
visa. An immigration document that allows you to enter a country.

Z
zygote intrafallopian transfer (ZIFT). A process where eggs are inseminated, then placed in the fallopian tubes.

zygote. An early embryo.

Appendix A:

Resources

This appendix provides numerous additional resources as you go through the process of building a family and dealing with the issues these decisions bring. In it you will find information on books, both for adults and children, organizations, and websites all designed to help your process be more informed and supported.

Books for Adults

ADOPTION TITLES

Adopting After Infertility
by Patricia Irwin Johnston

Adoption is a Family Affair!
What Relatives and Friends
Must Know
by Patricia Irwin Johnston

Adopting On Your Own:
The Complete Guide to Adoption
for Single Parents
by Lee Varon

Adoption Lifebook:
A Bridge to Your Child's Beginnings
by Cindy Probst

Breastfeeding the Adopted Baby
by Debra Stewart Peterson

How to Adopt Internationally:
A Guide for Agency-Directed and
Independent Adoptions
by Jean Nelson Erichsen and
Heino R. Erichsen

Is Adoption for You?:
The Information You Need to Make
the Right Choice
by Christine Adamec

Launching a Baby's Adoption:
Practical Strategies for Parents
and Professionals
by Patricia Irwin Johnston

Open Adoption Experience:
Complete Guide for Adoptive
and Birth Families
by Lois Ruskai Melina

Single Mothers by Choice:
A Guidebook for Single Women
Who Are Considering or
Have Chosen Motherhood
by Jane Mattes

Surrogate Motherhood:
Conception in the Heart
by Helena Ragone

Toddler Adoption:
The Weaver's Craft
by Mary Hopkins Best

Twenty Things Adopted Kids Wish
Their Adoptive Parents Knew
by Sherrie Eldridge

INFERTILITY TITLES

Alternative Beginnings:
A Woman's Guide to Getting
Pregnant by Self-Insemination
by Lisa Saffron

Choosing Assisted Reproduction:
Social, Emotional & Ethical
Considerations
by Susan Cooper

Choosing to Be Open
about Donor Conception
by Sharon Pettle and Ian Burns

Having a Baby Without a Man:
The Woman's Guide To
Alternative Insemination
by Susan Robinson, M.D. and
H.F. Pizer, P.A.C.

Helping the Stork:
The Choices and Challenges
of Donor Insemination
by Carol Frost Vercollone, et al

The Long-Awaited Stork:
A Guide to Parenting
After Infertility
by Ellen Sarasohn Glazer

Taking Charge of Infertility
by Patricia Irwin Johnston

Books for Children

ADOPTION TITLES

Adoption Is for Always
by Linda Walvoord Girard

The Best Single Mom in the World:
How I Was Adopted
by Mary Zisk

The Day We Met You
by Phoebe Koehler

Did My First Mother Love Me?
A Story for an Adopted Child
by Kathryn Ann Miller

Filling in the Blanks:
A Guided Look at
Growing Up Adopted
by Susan Gabel

Happy Adoption Day!
by John McCutcheon

Heart of Mine: A Story of Adoption
by Dan Hojer

How I Was Adopted
by Joanna Cole

I Love You Like Crazy Cakes
by Rose A. Lewis

Let's Talk About It: Adoption
by Fred Rogers

Mommy Far, Mommy Near:
An Adoption Story
by Carol Antoinette Peacock

My Special Family:
A Children's Book About
Open Adoption
by Kathleen Silber

Never Never Never
Will She Stop Loving You
by Jolene Durrant

Over the Moon: An Adoption Tale
by Karen Katz

Rosie's Family: An Adoption Story
by Lori Rosove

Seeds of Love:
For Brothers and Sisters
of International Adoption
by Mary Ebejer Petertyl

Two Birthdays for Beth
by Gay Lynn Cronin

We Wanted You
by Liz Rosenberg

When You Were Born in China:
A Memory Book for Children
Adopted from China
by Sara Dorow

When You Were Born in Korea
by Brian E. Boyd

Where Are My Birth Parents?:
A Guide for Teenage Adoptees
by Karen Gravelle

Who Am I?:
And Other Questions of Adopted
Kids (Plugged in)
by Charlene C. Giannetti

Why Was I Adopted?
by Carole Livingston

INFERTILITY TITLES

How Babies and Families Are Made:
There Is More Than One Way!
by Patricia Shaffer

How I Began:
The Story of Donor Insemination
by Julia Paul

Let Me Explain:
A Story About Donor Insemination
by Jane Schnitter

Mommy Did I Grow in Your Tummy?
Where Some Babies Come From
by Elaine R. Gordon

Phoebe's Family:
A Story about Egg Donation
by Linda Stamm

Magazines

Adoption TODAY Magazine
541 E. Garden Drive, Unit N
Windsor, CO 80550
888-924-6736
www.adoptinfo.net

Adoptive Families Magazine
42 West 38th St., Suite 901
New York, NY 10018
646-366-0830
www.adoptivefamilies.com

Organizations

American Academy of
Adoption Attorneys
P.O. Box 33053
Washington, DC 20033
202-832-2222
www.adoptionattorneys.org

Association of Administrators of the
Interstate Compact on
Adoption and Medical Assistance
810 First Street, N.E., Suite 500
Washington, DC 20002
202-682-0100
http://aaicama.aphsa.org

American Infertility Association
666 Fifth Avenue, Suite 278
New York, NY 10103
888-917-3777
www.americaninfertility.org

American Society for
Reproductive Medicine
1209 Montgomery Highway
Birmingham, Alabama 35216-2809
205-978-5000
www.asrm.org

FACE (Families Adopting
Children Everywhere)
Face, Inc.
P.O. Box 28058
Baltimore, MD 21239
410-488-2656 (Help-line)
www.faceadoptioninfo.org

Families for Private Adoption
P.O. Box 6375
Washington D.C. 20015-0375
202-722-0338
www.ffpa.org

Family Pride Coalition
P.O. Box 65327
Washington, D.C. 20035
202-231-5015
www.familypride.org

Generations United
1333 H Street, N.W.
Suite 500 W
Washington, D.C. 20005
202-289-3979
www.gu.org

Grandparents as Parents
P.O. 964
Lakewood, CA 90714
310-924-3996

International Concerns Committee
or Children
911 Cypress Drive
Boulder, CO 80303
303-494-8333
www.iccadopt.org

The International Council on Infertility
Information Dissemination, Inc.
P.O. Box 6836
Arlington, VA 22206
703-379-9178
www.inciid.org

Joint Council on
International Children's Services
1403 King Street
Suite 101
Alexandria, VA 22314
703-535-8045
www.jcics.org

National Adoption Assistance Training
Resource and Information Network
970 Raymond Avenue, Suite 106
St. Paul, MN 55114
800-470-6665

National Adoption Foundation
100 Mill Plain Rd.
Danbury, CT 06811
www.nafadopt.org/default.asp

National Adoption
Information Clearinghouse
330 C Street, SW
Washington, DC 20447
888-251-0075
703-352-3488
www.calib.com/naic

National Council for Adoption
225 N. Washington Street
Alexandria, VA 22314
703-299-6633
www.adoptioncouncil.org

*National Council for
Single Adoptive Parents*
P.O. Box 55
Wharton, NJ 07885
www.adopting.org/ncsap.html

*National Resource Center for Special
Needs Adoption*
16250 Northland Dr. Suite 120
Southfield, MI 48075
248-443-0306
www.nrcadoption.org/index.htm

*North American Council on
Adoptable Children*
970 Raymond Avenue Suite 106
St. Paul, MN 55114-1149
651-644-3036

*OPTS Organization of Parents
Through Surrogacy*
P.O. Box 611
Gurnee, IL 60031
847-782-0224
www.opts.com

*RESOLVE
The National Infertility Association*
1310 Broadway
Somerville MA 02144
888-623-0744
www.resolve.org

*Snowflakes
Nightlight Christian Adoptions*
801 E. Chapman, Ste 106
Fullerton, CA 92831
714-278-1020
www.snowflakes.org

Websites

Adoption Groups
www.adoptionintriad.org

Adoption Laws
www.law.cornell.edu/topics/
adoption.html

American Association of Tissue Banks
www.aath.org

*American Society of Reproductive
Medicine*
www.asrm.org

Adoption Online Support Group
www.adoptioncommunity.com

Adoption Support Group Database
www.adoptivefamilies.com/
support_group.php

*American Association of
Open Adoption Agencies*
www.openadoption.org

The American Surrogacy Center
(surrogacy and egg donor
information)
www.surrogacy.com

Association of Multiethnic Americans
www.ameasite.org

*Child of My Dreams: Adoption and
Infertility Support*
www.childofmydreams.com

*Children of Lesbians and
Gays Everywhere*
www.colage.org

Child Welfare League of America
www.cwla.org

Choosing an Adoption Agency
www.theadoptionguide.com/
adoption.php

ComeUnity Adoption Support
www.comeunity.com

Developmental Evaluators for
International Adoptions
www.calib.com/naic/pubs/
r_devev.cfm

Domestic versus International Adoption
www.adoptall.com/intguide.html

Egg Donor Agencies
www.everythingsurrogacy.com

Embryo Adoption
www.fertilityplus.org/faq/
donor.html#embryo

Everything Surrogacy
www.everythingsurrogacy.com

Families With Children From China
www.fcvn.org

Families with Children from Vietnam
www.fcvm.org

Foster Care Adoption
www.DaveThomasFoundationfor
Adoption.org

Gay and Lesbian friendly
adoption agencies
www.hrc.org/familynet/
adoption_groups.asp

Grandparent Kinship Adoption
Resources
www.calib.com/naic/pubs/
rl_dsp.cfm?subjID=30

National Embryo Donation Center
www.embryodonation.org

Home Insemination
www.fertilityplus.org

Home Study Agencies by State
**www.siblingsadoption.com/
homestudyagency.htm**

How to Make Adoption Affordable
www.nefe.org/adoption/index.html

Human Clone Rights Foundation
www.humanclonerights.org

Intended Parents.com
www.intendedparents.com

International Adoption Consortium
www.lacgrovp.org

International Adoptions
Finalized Abroad
www.calib.com/naic/laws/
international.cfm

IVF Connections Support
www.ivfconnections.com

In Vitro Maturation
www.fertilitytutorials.com

Joint Council of International
Children's Services
www.jcics.org

La leche League
www.laleche.org

Medicaid
www.cms.hhs.gov/medicaid

National Adoption
Information Clearinghouse
(division of the U.S Department of
Health and Human Services)
www.calib.com/naic

National Dissemination Center
for Children w/ Disabilities
www.nichcy.org

Offspring: for children seeking
sperm donor parents
www.cbc.ca/programs/sites/
features/offspring/index.htm

Older Child Adoption
www.olderchildadoption.com

Online Infertility Support Groups
www.surrogacy.com/group/
ogroups.html

Open Adoption Resources
www.r2press.com

Reprotech
(embryo donation info)
www.reprot.com

Single Parent Adoption Network
http://members.aol.com/
Onemomfor2

Sperm Bank Directory
www.spermbankdirectory.com

Sperm Bank List
www.fertilityplus.org/faq/
donor.html#sperm

State Child Welfare Agencies and
Photolisting Sites
www.calib.com/naic/pubs/
r_agency.cfm

Surrogate Mothers Online
www.surromomsonline.com

U.S. Adoption laws by state
www.abcadoptions.com/uslaw.htm

U.S. Department of State
http://travel.state.gov/adopt.html

U.S. photolistings
www.adoptuskids.org/servlet/
page?_pageid=65&_dad=
portal30&_schema=PORTAL30

U.S. Adoption

STATE INSTRUCTIONS AND EXPLANATIONS

Missouri:
www.mobar.org/pamphlet/
adoption2.htm

Tennessee:
http://harmony.cc/resource/law/
tnalo.pdf

Vermont:
www.state.vt.us/srs/adoption/
handbook2003.pdf

Wisconsin:
www.dhfs.state.wi.us/children/
adoption

Appendix B:

State Offices for Adoption Services

Each state has a governmental office that oversees the adoption process of that state. This office may be designed to place children who have become wards of the state up for adoption, but often this office can provides a vast amount of information for families wanting to adopt privately and even internationally. This state office is also the entity that will conduct the home study when you are going through the placement process.

This appendix contains each state's office for handling adoption along with its contact information. Nearly every state's office has a website so you can gather even more information that is specific to your state on that site.

ALABAMA
Alabama Department of Human Resources
Family Services Division,
Office of Adoption
50 North Ripley Street
Montgomery, AL 36130-4000
334-242-1374
www.dhr.state.al.us/fsd/adopt.asp

ALASKA
Alaska Department of Health and Social Services
Division of Family and Youth Services
350 Main Street, 4th Floor,
P.O. Box 110630
Juneau, AK 99811-0630
907-465-2145
www.hss.state.ak.us/dfys

ARIZONA
Arizona Department of Economic Security
Children, Youth & Families Division
P.O. Box 6123, Site Code 940A
Phoenix, AZ 85005
602-542-5499

ARKANSAS
Arkansas Department of Human Services
Division of Children and Family Services
P.O. Box 1437, Slot 808
Little Rock, AR 72203-1437
501-682-8462
Toll Free: (888) 736-2820
www.state.ar.us/dhs/adoption/adoption.html

CALIFORNIA
California Department of Social Services
Child and Youth Permanency Branch
744 P Street, MS 19-69
Sacramento, CA 95814
916-323-2921
800-543-7487
www.childsworld.ca.gov

COLORADO

Colorado Department of Human Services
1575 Sherman Street
Denver, CO 80203-1714
303-866-3197

CONNECTICUT

Connecticut Department of Children and Families
Office of Adoption and Foster Care Services
505 Hudson Street
Hartford, CT 06106
860-550-6350
www.state.ct.us/dcf/foster.htm

DELAWARE

Delaware Department of Services for Children, Youth and Their Families
1825 Faulkland Road
Wilmington, DE 19805-1195
302-633-2655
www.state.de.us/kids/adoption.htm

DISTRICT OF COLUMBIA

District of Columbia Child and Family Services
William Johnson
400 6th Street
Washington, DC 20024
202-727-4733

FLORIDA

Florida Department of Children and Families
1317 Winewood Boulevard, Building 7
Tallahassee, FL 32399-0700
850-921-2177
http://www5.myflorida.com/cf_web/myflorida2/healthhuman/adoption

GEORGIA

Georgia Department of Human Resources
Division of Children and Family Services, Office of Adoptions
2 Peachtree Street NW,
Suite 3-323
Atlanta, GA 30303-3142
404-657-3558

HAWAII

Hawaii Department of Human Services
810 Richards Street, Suite 400
Honolulu, HI 96813
808-586-5698
www.state.hi.us/dhs/index.html

IDAHO

Idaho Department of Health and Welfare
Division of Family and Community Services
P.O. Box 83720, 450 West State Street
Boise, ID 83720-0036
208-334-5700
http://www2.state.id.us/dhw/Adoption

ILLINOIS

Illinois Department of Children and Family Services
Division of Foster Care and Permanency Services
406 East Monroe Street, Station 25
Springfield, IL 62701-1498
217-524-2422
www.state.il.us/dcfs

INDIANA

Indiana Division of Family and Children
Bureau of Family Protection and Preservation
402 West Washington Street,
3rd Floor, W-364
Indianapolis, IN 46204
317-232-4622
www.in.gov/fssa/adoption/index.html

IOWA

Iowa Department of Human Services
Adult, Children and Family Services
Hoover State Office Building,
5th Floor
Des Moines, IA 50319
515-281-5358
www.dhs.state.ia.us/ACFS/ACFS.asp

KANSAS

Kansas Department of Social and Rehabilitation Services
Children and Family Policy Division
915 SW Harrison, 5th Floor
Topeka, KS 66612
785-296-0918
www.srskansas.org

KENTUCKY

Commonwealth of Kentucky
Cabinet for Families & Children
275 East Main Street, 3CE
Franford, KY 40621
502-564-2147
http://cfc.state.ky.us/help/adoption.asp

LOUISIANA

Louisiana Department of Social Services
Office of Community Services
5700 Florida Boulevard, 8th Floor,
P.O. Box 3318
Baton Rouge, LA 70821
225-216-6925
www.dss.state.la.us

MAINE

Maine Department of Human Services
Bureau of Child and Family Services
221 State Street, State House Station #111
Augusta, ME 04333-0011
207-287-5062
www.adoptuskids.org/states/me

MARYLAND

Maryland Department of Human Resources
Social Services Administration
311 W. Saratoga Street
Baltimore, MD 21201
410-767-7506
www.dhr.state.md.us/adopt.htm

MASSACHUSETTS

Massachusetts Department of Social Services
24 Farnsworth Street
Boston, MA 02210
617-748-2267
www.state.ma.us/dss/Adoption/AD_Overview.htm

MICHIGAN

Michigan Family Independence Agency
Child and Family Services Administration
P.O. Box 30037, Suite 413
Lansing, MI 48909
517-373-3513
www.mfia.state.mi.us/cfsadmin/adoption/adoption.html

MINNESOTA

Minnesota Department of Human Services
Children's Services
444 Lafayette Road North, Human Services Building
St. Paul, MN 55155-3831
651-296-3740
www.dhs.state.mn.us/childint/programs/Adoption/default.htm

MISSISSIPPI

Mississippi Department of Human Services
Division of Family and Child Services
750 N State Street
Jackson, MS 39202
601-359-4981
www.mdhs.state.ms.us/fcs_adopt.html

MISSOURI

Missouri Department of Social Services
Division of Family Services
P.O. Box 88
Jefferson City, MO 65103
573-751-0311
www.dss.state.mo.us/dfs/adopt.htm

MONTANA

Montana Department of Public Health and Human Services
Child and Family Services Division
P.O. Box 8005
Helena, MT 59604-8005
406-444-5919
www.dphhs.state.mt.us

NEBRASKA

Nebraska Department of Health and Human Services
P.O. Box 95044
Lincoln, NE 68509-5044
402-471-9331
www.hhs.state.ne.us/adp/adpindex.htm

NEVADA

Nevada Department of Human Resources
Division of Child and Family Services
6171 West Charleston Boulevard, Building 15
Las Vegas, NV 89102
702-486-7633
http://dcfs.state.nv.us/page33.html

NEW HAMPSHIRE

New Hampshire Department of Health and Human Services
Division for Children, Youth and Families
129 Pleasant Street
Concord, NH 03301
603-271-4707

NEW JERSEY

New Jersey Department of Human Services
Division of Youth and Family Services
50 East State Street, 5th Floor, CN 717
Trenton, NJ 08625-0717
609-984-2380
www.state.nj.us/humanservices/adoption/adopt.html

NEW MEXICO

Central Adoption Unit
P.O. Drawer 5160
Santa Fe, NM 87502-5160
505-841-7949
www.state.nm.us/cyfd/foster.htm

NEW YORK

New York State Department of Family Assistance
Office of Children and Family Services
40 North Pearl Street, Riverview Center, 6th Floor
Albany, NY 12243
518-474-9406
www.dfa.state.ny.us

NORTH CAROLINA

*North Carolina Department of
Health and Human Services
Division of Social Services,
Children's Services Section*
2408 Mial Service Center
Raleigh, NC 27699-2408
919-733-4622
www.dhhs.state.nc.us/dss/adopt

NORTH DAKOTA

North Dakota Department of Human Services
600 East Boulevard Avenue
Bismarck, ND 58505
701-328-4805
www.state.nd.us/humanservices

OHIO

*Ohio Bureau of Family Services
Office for Children and Families*
255 East Main Street, 4th Floor
Columbus, OH 43215
614-466-9274
http://jfs.ohio.gov

OKLAHOMA

*Oklahoma Department of Human Services
Division of Children and Family Services*
P.O. Box 25352, 2400 North Lincoln Blvd
Oklahoma City, OK 73125
405-521-2475
www.okdhs.org/adopt

OREGON

Oregon Department of Human Services
800 N.E. Oregon Street
Portland, OR 97232
800-422-6012
503-945-5677
www.dhs.state.or.us/children/adoption

PENNSYLVANIA

Pennsylvania Department of Public Welfare
Office of Children, Youth and Families
P.O. Box 2675, 7th & Forster Street
Harrisburg, PA 17105-2675
717-705-2912
www.dpw.state.pa.us/ocyf/ocyfas.asp

RHODE ISLAND

Rhode Island Department of Children, Youth and Families
530 Wood Street
Bristol, RI 02805
401-254-7010
www.adoptionri.org

SOUTH CAROLINA

South Carolina Department of Social Services
Division of Human Services
P.O. Box 1520
Columbia, SC 29202-1520
803-898-7707
www.state.sc.us/dss/adoption

SOUTH DAKOTA

South Dakota Department of Social Services
Child Protection Services
700 Governor's Drive, Kneip Building
Pierre, SD 57501-2291
605-773-3227
www.state.sd.us/social/cps/adoption/index.htm

TENNESSEE

Tennessee Department of Children's Services
436 Sixth Avenue North, Cordell Hull Building, 8th Floor
Nashville, TN 37243-1290
615-532-5637
www.state.tn.us/youth/adoption

TEXAS

Texas Department of Protective and Regulatory Services
P.O. Box 149030, E-557
Austin, TX 78717-9030
512-438-4516
www.tdprs.state.tx.us

UTAH

Utah Department of Human Services
Division of Child and Family Services
120 North, 200 West, P.O. Box 45500
Salt Lake City, UT 84103
801-538-4078
www.hsdcfs.state.ut.us

VERMONT

Vermont Department of Social and Rehabilitation Services
103 South Main Street
Waterbury, VT 05671
802-241-2142
www.state.vt.us/srs/adoption/index.html

VIRGINIA

Virginia Department Of Social Services
Division of Family Services
730 East Broad Street
Richmond, VA 21219-1849
804-692-1290
www.dss.state.va.us/family/adoption.html

WASHINGTON

Washington Department of Social and Health Services
Children's Administration
P.O. Box 45713
Olympia, WA 98504
360-902-7959
360-902-7968
www.wa.gov/dshs/ca/ca3ov.html

WEST VIRGINIA

West Virginia Department of Health and Human Resources
Office of Social Services
350 Capitol Street, Room 621
Charleston, WV 25301-3704
304-558-4303
www.wvdhhr.org/oss/children/adoption.htm

WISCONSIN

Wisconsin Department of Health and Family Services
Division of Child and Family Services
P.O. Box 8916
Madison, WI 53708-8916
608-266-3595
www.dhfs.state.wi.us/children/adoption/index.htm

WYOMING

Wyoming Department of Family Services
2300 Capitol Avenue, Hathaway Building, 3rd Floor, Room 376
Cheyenne, WY 82002-0490
307-777-3570
http://dfsweb.state.wy.us/childsvc/toc1.htm

Appendix C:

Forms

The following forms will be useful for different adoption and fertility arrangements. You can also find the adoption forms online at *http://uscis.gov.*

INSEMINATION AGREEMENT

This agreement is made on _____ (date) between the parties _____ (the donor) and _____ (the recipient).

1. The parties are both single and never married.

2. The donor agrees to provide semen to the recipient for use in artificial insemination.

3. The parties agree that the semen may be frozen and saved for future use and may also be used immediately.

4. The recipient agrees to pay the donor $_____ for each semen donation he makes under the terms of this agreement.

5. The parties agree that the donor is making donations for use by the recipient in her attempts to become pregnant. The recipient plans to use artificial insemination of the donor's semen during the following time period _____ to become pregnant.

6. The donor is donating semen for the recipient's use and agrees not to seek custody, visitation, guardianship or contact with any child that results from the insemination. He hereby waives any and all parental rights now or in the future and waives any right as to the names of the children resulting from the insemination.

7. The donor agrees that she has no right to seek financial assistance from the donor and waives all rights to child support, confinement expenses or birth expenses for herself or any resulting child.

8. Both parties agree not to seek a determination of paternity of any child resulting from the insemination in any court or tribunal and waive any right to any such determination of paternity.

9. The parties agree that the birth certificates for any children resulting from the insemination will not name a father and specifically will not name the donor in any capacity.

10. The parties agree to use a licensed physician to perform the insemination. This is in compliance with _____ (fill in state law if applicable) to avoid the donor being named as the legal father of the child.

initial: _____   _____

11. The identity of the donor will be kept secret by both the donor and recipient and will not be revealed with consent of the other party.

12. The recipient shall have the right to choose a guardian for any children resulting from the insemination. The recipient shall also have the right to consent to a second parent adoption of any children resulting from the insemination. Donor shall in no way interfere with any of these procedures, determinations or exercises of rights.

13. The parties agree that the termination of rights stated in this agreement are permanent and irrevocable. Neither party may institute any court proceeding involving custody, visitation, guardianship, paternity or child support against the other with respect to the children resulting from the insemination.

14. Donor agrees not to have any contact with any children resulting from the insemination without the express knowing consent of the recipient. The parties agree that any contact between donor and the resulting children shall in no way alter, impact or effect the terms of this agreement or the legal relationship of the parties. Any contact that may occur will in no way be seen as implying or allowing donor the right to obtain, seek or ask for parental rights or responsibilities.

15. The parties make this agreement willingly and freely, under no duress. Both parties have been advised to seek separate legal counsel before executing this document.

16. The parties understand each and every provision of this agreement. The agreement contains the entire agreement made between the parties and there are no other promises, understandings or agreements between the parties other than what is contained herein.

17. The numbered provisions of this agreement may be enforced separately and individually by both parties.

18. This agreement is made pursuant to the laws of _____ (your state) and will be enforced according to the laws of that state.

initial: _____   _____

19. The parties agree that this agreement can only be altered in writing and must be signed by both parties to become valid.

_____   _____   _____

Donor Name   Donor Signature   Date

_____   _____   _____

Recipient Name   Recipient Signature   Date

Notary:

Petition to Classify Orphan as an Immediate Relative

Eligibility.

Child. Under immigration law, an orphan is an alien child who has no parents because of the death or disappearance of, abandonment or desertion by, or separation or loss from both parents. An orphan is also a child who has only one parent who is not capable of taking care of the orphan and who has, in writing, irrevocably released the orphan for emigration and adoption. A petition to classify an alien as an orphan may not be filed in behalf of a child in the United States, unless that child is in parole status and has not been adopted in the United States. The petition must be filed before the child's 16th birthday.

Parent(s). The petition may be filed by a married United States citizen and spouse or unmarried United States citizen at least twenty-five years of age. The spouse does not need to be a United States citizen.

Adoption abroad. If the orphan was adopted abroad, it must be established that both the married petitioner and spouse or the unmarried petitioner personally saw and observed the child prior to or during the adoption proceedings. The adoption decree must show that a married petitioner and spouse adopted the child jointly or that an unmarried petitioner was at least 25 years of age at the time of the adoption.

Proxy adoption abroad. If both the petitioner and spouse or the unmarried petitioner did not personally see and observe the child prior to or during the adoption proceedings abroad, the petitioner (and spouse, if married) must submit a statement indicating the petitioner's (and, if married, the spouse's) willingness and intent to readopt the child in the United States. If requested, the petitioner must submit a statement by an official of the state in which the child will reside that readoption is permissible in that state. In addition, evidence of compliance with the preadoption requirements, if any, of that state must be submitted.

E. Preadoption requirements. If the orphan has not been adopted abroad, the petitioner and spouse or the unmarried petitioner must establish that the child will be adopted in the United States by the petitioner and spouse jointly or by the unmarried petitioner and that the preadoption requirement, if any, of the state of the orphan's proposed residence have been met.

2. Filing petition for known child.

An orphan petition for a child who has been identified must be submitted on a completed Form I-600 with the certification of petitioner executed and the required fee. If the petitioner is married, the Form I-600 must also be signed by the petitioner's spouse. The petition must be accompanied by the following:

A. Proof of United States citizenship of the petitioner.

(1) If the petitioner is a citizen by reason of birth in the United States, submit a copy of the petitioner's birth certificate, or if birth certificate is unobtainable, a copy of petitioner's baptismal certificate under the seal of the church, showing place of birth, (baptism must have occurred within two months after birth), or if a birth or baptismal certificate cannot be obtained, affidavits of two United States citizens who have personal knowledge of petitioner's birth in the United States.

(2) If the petitioner was born outside the United States and became a citizen through the naturalization or citizenship of a parent or husband and and has not been issued a certificate of citizenship in his or her own name, submit evidence of the citizenship and marriage of the parent or husband, as well as termination of any prior marriages.

Also, if petitioner claims citizenship through a parent, submit petitioner's birth certificate and a separate statement showing the date, place, and means of all his or her arrivals and departures into and out of the United States.

(3) If petitioner's naturalization occurred within 90 days immediately preceding the filing of this petition, or if it occurred prior to September 27, 1906, the naturalization certificate must accompany the petition.

(4) An unexpired U.S. passport initially issued for ten years may also be submitted.

B. **Proof of marriage of petitioner and spouse.**
The married petitioner should submit a certificate of the marriage and proof of termination of all prior marriages of himself or herself and spouse. In the case of an unmarried petitioner who was previously married, submit proof of termination of all prior marriages. **NOTE:** If any change occurs in the petitioner's marital status while the case is pending, the district director should be notified immediately.

C. **Proof of age of orphan.**
Petitioner should submit a copy of the orphan's birth certificate if obtainable; if not obtainable, submit an explanation together with the best available evidence of birth.

D. **Copies of the death certificate(s) of the child's parent(s), if applicable.**

E. **A certified copy of adoption decree together with certified translation,** if the orphan has been lawfully adopted abroad.

F. **Evidence that the sole or surviving parent is incapable of providing for the orphan's care** and has, in writing, irrevocably released the orphan for emigration and adoption, if the orphan has only one parent.

G. **Evidence that the orphan has been unconditionally abandoned to an orphanage,** if the orphan has been placed in an orphanage by his/her parent or parents.

H. **Evidence that the preadoption requirements, i**
of the state of the orphan's proposed residen
have been met, if the child is to be adopted in
United States. If it is not possible to submit ■
evidence upon initial filing of the petition und■
laws of the state of proposed residence, it ma
submitted later. The petition, however, will n■
approved without it.

I. **A home study** with a statement or attachment
recommending or approving of the adoption or
proposed adoption signed by an official of the
responsible state agency in the state of the ch■
proposed residence or of an agency authorized
that state, or, in the case of a child adopted
abroad, of an appropriate public or private ado■
agency which is licensed in the United States.
Both individuals and organizations may qualify
agencies. If the recommending agency is a
licensed agency, the recommendation must se■
forth that it is licensed, the state in which it is
licensed, its license number, if any, and the pe■
of validity of its license. The research, includi■
interviewing, however, and the preparation of
home study may be done by an individual or g
in the United States or abroad satisfactory to ■
recommending agency. A responsible state ag
or licensed agency can accept a home study n
by an unlicensed agency can accept a home st■
made by an unlicensed or foreign agency and ■
that home study as a basis for a favorable
recommendation. The home study must conta
but is not limited to, the following elements:

(1) the financial ability of the adoptive or
prospective parent or parents to read a■
educate the child.

(2) a detailed description of the living
accommodations where the adoptive or
prospective parent or parents currently

(3) a detailed description of the living
accommodations where the child will re

(4) a factual evaluation of the physical, men■
moral capabilities of the adoptive or prosp■
parent or parents in relation to rearing an■
educating the child.

Fingerprints.

Each member of the married prospective adoptive couple or the married prospective adoptive parent, and each additional adult member of the prospective adoptive parents' household must be fingerprinted in connection with this petition.

Petitioners residing in the United States. After filing this petition, INS will notify each person in writing of the time and location where they must go to be fingerprinted. Failure to appear to be fingerprinted may result in denial of the petition.

Petitioners residing abroad. Completed fingerprint cards (Forms FD-258) must be submitted with the petition. Do not bend, fold, or crease completed fingerprint cards. Fingerprint cards must be prepared by a United States consular office or a United States military installation.

┃ing Petition for Known Child Without Full ┃cumentation on Child or Home Study.

┃hen a child has been identified but the documentary ┃idence relating to him/her or the home study is not ┃t available, an orphan petition may be filed without ┃at evidence or home study. The evidence outlined in ┃structions 2A and 2B, however, must be submitted. ┃ the necessary evidence relating to the child or the ┃me study is not submitted within one year from the ┃te of submission of the petition, the petition will be ┃nsidered abandoned and the fee will not be refunded. ┃ny further proceeding will require the filing of a new ┃tition.

┃bmitting an Application for Advance ┃ocessing of an Orphan Petition in Behalf ┃ a Child Who Has Not Been Identified.

┃ prospective petitioner may request advance ┃ocessing when the child has not been identified or ┃en the prospective petitioner and/or spouse are or is ┃ing abroad to locate or adopt a child. If unmarried, ┃e prospective petitioner must be at least 24 years of ┃e, provided that he or she will be at least 25 at the ┃ne of the adoption and the completed petition in ┃half of a child is filed. The request must be on Form ┃00A, Application for Advance Processing of Orphan ┃tition, and must be accompanied by the evidence ┃quired by that form. After a child or children are ┃cated and/or identified, a separate Form I-600, ┃tition to Classify Orphan as an Immediate Relative, ┃ust be filed for each child. A new fee is not required ┃only one Form I-600 is filed, provided the form is filed ┃thin one year of completion of all advance

processing in a case where there has been a favorable determination concerning the prospective petitioner's ability to care for a beneficiary orphan.

5. When Child/Children Located and/or Identified.

A separate form I-600, Petition to Classify Orphan as an Immediate Relative, must be filed for each child. A new fee is not required if only one form I-600 is filed and it is filed within one year of completion of all advance processing in a case where there has been a favorable determination concerning the beneficiary orphan.

Normally, Form I-600 should be submitted to the INS office where the advance processing application was filed. The Immigration and Naturalization Service has offices in the following countries: Austria, China, Cuba, Denmark, Dominican Republic, Ecuador, El Salvador, Germany, Ghana, Great Britain, Greece, Guatemala, Haiti, Honduras, India, Italy, Jamaica, Kenya, Korea, Mexico, Pakistan, Panama, Peru, Philippines, Russia, Singapore, South Africa, Spain, Thailand, and Vietnam. A prospective petitioner who is going abroad to adopt or locate a child in one of these countries should file Form I-600 at the INS office having jurisdiction over the place where the child is residing or will be located unless the case is being retained at the stateside office.

However, a prospective petitioner who is going abroad to any other country to adopt or locate a child should file Form I-600 at the American embassy or consulate having jurisdiction over the place where the child is residing or wil be located unless the case is being retained at the stateside office.

The case may be retained at the stateside office, if the petitioner requests it and if it appears that the case will be processed more quickly in that manner. Form I-600 must be accompanied by all the evidence required on the instruction sheet of that form, except that the evidence required by and submitted with this form need not be furnished.

6. General Filing Instructions.

A. Type or print legibly in ink.

B. If extra space is needed to complete any item, attach a continuation sheet, indicate the item number, and date and sign each sheet.

C. **Translations.** Any foreign language document must be accompanied by a full English translation, which the translator has certified as complete and correct, and by the translator's certification that he or she is competent to translate the foreign language into English.

D. **Copies.** If these instruction state that a copy of a document may be filed with this petition and you choose to send us the original, we may keep that original for our records.

7. Submission of petition.

A petitioner residing in the United States should send the completed petition to the INS office having jurisdiction over his/her place of residence. A petitioner residing outside the United States should consult the nearest American embassy or consulate designated to act on the petition.

8. Fee. Read instructions carefully.

A fee of four hundred and sixty dollars ($460) must be submitted for filing this petition. There is a fifty dollar ($50) per person, fingerprinting fee, in addition to the petition fee for each person residing in the United States and required to be fingerprinted. For example, if a petition is filed by a married couple residing in the United States with one additional adult member in their household, the total of fees that must be submitted is $610. However, if a petition is filed by a married couple residing abroad, only the petition fee of $460 must be submitted.

One check or money order may be submitted for both the petition fee and the fingerprinting fees. It cannot be refunded regardless of the action taken on the petition. **Do not mail cash. All fees must be submitted in the exact amount.** Payment by a check or money order must be drawn on a bank or other institution located in the United States and be payable in United States currency.

If the petitioner resides in Guam, the check or money order must be payable to the "Treasurer, Guam."

If the petitioner resides in the Virgin Islands, check or money order must be payable to the "Commissioner of Finance of the Virgin Islands."

All other petitioners must make the check or money order payable to the "Immigration and Naturalization Service." When a check is drawn on the account of a person other than the petitioner, the name of the petitioner must be entered on the face of the check.

If petition is submitted from outside the United St remittance may be made by a bank international m order or foreign draft drawn on a financial instituti the United States and payable to the Immigration Naturalization Service in United States currency. Personal checks are accepted subject to collectibi An uncollectible check in payment of a petition fe render the petition and any document issued inval charge of $30.00 will be imposed if a check in pa of a fee is not honored by the bank on which it is drawn. When more than one petition is submitted the same petitioner in behalf of orphans who are siblings, only one set of petition and fingerprinting is required.

9. Assistance.

Assistance may be obtained from a recognized agency or from any public or private agency. T following recognized social agencies, which hav offices in many of the principal cities of the Uni States, have agreed to furnish assistance:

Bethany Christian Services.
2600 Fivemile Road NE
Grand Rapids, MI. 419525
Tel: (616) 224-7446
Fax: (616) 224-7585

Catholic Legal Immigration Network, Inc., (CL
415 Michigan Avenue, NE., Suite 150
Washington, DC 20017
Tel: (202) 635-2556
Fax: (202) 635-2649

International Social Services/U.S. of America Branch
700 Light Street
Baltimore, MD. 21230
Tel: (410) 230-2734
Fax: (410) 230-2741

United States Catholic Conference Migration Refugee Services (USCC/MRS).
3211 4th Street, NE
Washington, DC 20017
Tel: (202) 541-3352
Fax: (202) 722-8800

10. Penalties.

Willful false statements on this form or supportir documents can be punished by fine or imprisonm U.S. Code, Title 18, Sec. 1001 (formerly Sec. 8(

Authority.

8 USC 1154(a). Routine uses for disclosure under the Privacy Act of 1974 have been published in the Federal Register and are available upon request. INS will use the information to determine immigrant eligibility. Submission of the information is voluntary, but failure to provide any or all of the information may result in denial of the petition.

Reporting Burden.

A person is not required to respond to a collection of information unless it displays a currently valid OMB control number. Public reporting burden for this collection of information is estimated to average 30 minutes per response, including the time for reviewing instructions, searching existing data sources, gathering and maintaining the data needed, and completing and reviewing the collection of information. Send comments regarding this burden estimate or any other aspect of this collection of information, including suggestions for reducing this burden, to: Immigration and Naturalization Service, HQPDI, 425 I Street, N.W., Room 4034, Washington, DC 20536; OMB No. 1115-0049. **DO NOT MAIL YOUR COMPLETED APPLICATION TO THIS ADDRESS.**

Petition to Classify Orphan

an Immediate Relative

U.S. Department of Justice

Immigration and Naturalization Service

[Section 101 (b)(1)(F) of the Immigration and Nationality Act, as amende...

Please do not write in this block.

TO THE SECRETARY OF STATE;

The petition was filed by:

☐ Married petitioner   ☐ Unmarried petitioner

The petition is approved for orphan:

☐ Adopted abroad   ☐ Coming to U.S. for adoption.
Preadoption requirements have
been met.

Fee Stamp

Remarks:

File number

DATE OF
ACTION

DD

DISTRICT

Please type or print legibly in ink. Use a separate petition for each child.

Petition is being made to classify the named orphan as an immediate relative.

BLOCK I - Information about prospective

1. My name is: (Last)   (First)   (Middle)

2. Other names used (including maiden name if appropriate):

3. I reside in the U.S.   (C/O if appropriate)   (Apt. No.)

   (Number and street)   (Town or city)   (State)   (Zip Code)

4. Address abroad (if any)(Number and street)   (Apt. No.)

   (Town or city)   (Province)   (Country)

5. I was born on: (Month)   (Day)   (Year)

   In: (Town or City)   (State or Province)   (Country)

6. My phone number is: (Include Area Code)

7. My marital status is:

   ☐ Married
   ☐ Widowed
   ☐ Divorced
   ☐ Single
       ☐ I have never been married.
       ☐ I have been previously married _____ time(s).

8. If you are now married, give the following information:

Date and place of present marriage

Name of present spouse (include maiden name of wife)

Date of birth of spouse   Place of birth of spouse

Number of prior marriages of spouse

My spouse resides ☐ With me   ☐ Apart from me
                                   (provide address belov...

(Apt. No.)   (No. and street)   (City)   (State)   (Coun...

9. I am a citizen of the United States through:

   ☐ Birth   ☐ Parents   ☐ Naturalization

If acquired through naturalization, give name under which
naturalized, number of naturalization certificate, and date and
place of naturalization:

If not, submit evidence of citizenship. See Instruction 2.a(2).

If acquired through parentage, have you obtained a certificate i...
your own name based on that acquisition?

☐ No   ☐ Yes

Have you or any person through whom you claimed citizenship
ever lost United States citizenship?

☐ No   ☐ Yes (If yes, attach detailed explanation.)

Continue on reve...

Received	Trans. In	Ret'd Trans. Out	Complete

Form I-600 (Rev. 11/28/01)Y

BLOCK II - Information about orphan beneficiary

10. Name at birth   (First)   (Middle)   (Last)

11. Name at present   (First)   (Middle)   (Last)

12. Any other names by which orphan is or was known.

13. Sex   ☐ Male   14. Date of birth (Month/Day/Year)
      ☐ Female

15. Place of birth (City)   (State or Province)   (Country)

16. The beneficiary is an orphan because (check One)
   ☐ He/she has no parents.
   ☐ He/she has only one parent who is the sole or surviving

17. If the orphan has only one parent, answer the following
   a. State what has become of the other parent:

   b. Is the remaining parent capable of providing for the orphan's
     support?   ☐ Yes   ☐ No
   c. Has the remaining parent, in writing, irrevocably released
     orphan for emigration and adoption? ☐ Yes   ☐ No

18. Has the orphan been adopted abroad by the petitioner and
jointly or the unmarried petitioner?   ☐ Yes   ☐ No

   If yes, did the petitioner and spouse or unmarried petitioner
   personally see and observe the child prior to or during the
   adoption proceedings?   ☐ Yes   ☐ No

   Date of adoption

   Place of adoption

19. If either answer in question 18 is "No", answer the following:
   a. Do petitioner and spouse jointly or does the unmarried
     intend to adopt the orphan in the United States?
      ☐ Yes   ☐ No
   b. Have the preadoption requirements, if any, of the orphan's
     proposed state of residence been met?
      ☐ Yes   ☐ No
   c. If b. is answered "No", will they be met later?
      ☐ Yes   ☐ No

20. To petitioner's knowledge, does the orphan have any physical or
affliction?   ☐ Yes   ☐ No
If "Yes", name the affliction.

21. Who has legal custody of the child?

22. Name of child welfare agency, if any, assisting in this case:

23. Name of attorney abroad, if any, representing petitioner in this

   Address of above.

24. Address in the United States where orphan will reside.

25. Present address of orphan.

25. If orphan is residing in an institution, give full name of institution.

26. If orphan is not residing in an institution, give full name of person
   whom orphan is residing.

27. Give any additional information necessary to locate orphan such
   as name of district, section, zone or locality in which orphan
   resides.

28. Location of American Consulate where application for visa will
be made.
   (City in Foreign Country)   (Foreign Country)

Certification of prospective petitioner

I certify under penalty of perjury under the laws of the United States of America that the foregoing is true and correct and that I will care for an orphan/orphans properly if admitted to the United States.

(Signature of Prospective Petitioner)

Executed on (Date)

Certification of married prospective petitioner's spouse

I certify under penalty of perjury under the laws of the United States of America that the foregoing is true and correct and that my spouse and I will care for an orphan/orphans properly if admitted to the United States.

(Signature of Prospective Petitioner)

Executed on (Date)

Signature of person preparing form, if other than petitioner

I declare that this document was prepared by me at the request of the prospective petitioner and is based on all information of which I have any knowledge.

(Signature)

Address

Executed on (Date)

U.S. Department of Justice
Immigration and Naturalization Service

Application for Advance Processing of Orphan Petition (8CFR 204.1(b)(3))

Advanced processing is a procedure for completing the part of an orphan petition relating to the petitioner before an orphan is located so that there will be no unnecessary delays in processing the petition after an orphan is located.
USE THIS FORM ONLY IF YOU WISH TO ADOPT AN ORPHAN WHO HAS NOT YET BEEN LOCATED AND IDENTIFIED OR YOU AND/OR YOUR SPOUSE, IF MARRIED, ARE/IS GOING ABROAD TO ADOPT OR LOCATE A CHILD.
This application is not a petition to classify orphan as an immediate relative (Form I-600).

1. Eligibility.

A. Eligibility for advance processing application (Form I-600A). An application for advance processing may be filed by a married United States citizen and spouse. The spouse does not need to be a United States citizen. It may also be filed by an unmarried United States citizen at least 24 years of age provided that he or she will be at least 25 at the time of the adoption and of filing an orphan petition in behalf of a child.

B. Eligibility for Orphan Petition (Form I-600). In addition to the requirements concerning the citizenship and age of the petitioner described in Instruction 1a, when a child is located and identified, the following eligibility requirements will apply:

(1) **Child.** Under immigration law, an orphan is an alien child who has no parents because of the death or disappearance of, abandonment or desertion by, or separation or loss from both parents. An orphan is also a child who has only one parent who is not capable of taking care of the orphan and who has, in writing, irrevocably released the orphan for emigration and adoption. A petition to classify an alien as an orphan may not be filed in behalf of a child in the United States unless that child is in parole status and has not been adopted in the United States. The petition must be filed before the child's 16th birthday.

(2) **Adoption abroad.** If the orphan was adopted abroad, it must be established that both the married petitioner and spouse or the unmarried petitioner personally saw and observed the child prior to or during the adoption proceedings. The adoption decree must show that a married petitioner and spouse adopted the child jointly or that an unmarried petitioner was at least 25 years of age at the time of the adoption.

(3) **Proxy adoption abroad.** If both the petitioner and spouse or the unmarried petitioner did not personally see and observe the child prior to or during the adoption proceedings abroad, the petitioner (and spouse, if married) must submit a statement indicating the petitioner's (and, if married, the spouse's) willingness and intent to readopt the child in the United States. If requested, the petitioner must submit a statement by an official of the state in which the child will reside that readoption is permissible in that state. In addition, evidence of compliance with the preadoption requirements, if any, of that state must be submitted.

(4) **Preadoption requirements.** If the orphan has not been adopted abroad, the petitioner and spouse or the unmarried petitioner must establish that the child will be adopted in the United States by the petitioner and spouse jointly or by the unmarried petitioner and that the preadoption requirement, if any, of the state of the orphan's proposed residence have been met.

2. Filing Advance Processing Application.

An advance processing application must be submitted on Form I-600A with the certification of prospective petitioner executed and the required fee. If the prospective petitioner is married, the Form I-600A must also be signed by the prospective petitioner's spouse. The application must be accompanied by:

Proof of United States citizenship of the prospective petitioner.

If the petitioner is a citizen by reason of birth in the United States, submit a copy of the petitioner's birth certificate, or if birth certificate is unobtainable, a copy of petitioner's baptismal certificate under seal of the church, showing place of birth, (baptism must have occurred within two months after birth), or if a birth or baptismal certificate cannot be obtained, affidavits of two United States citizens who have personal knowledge of petitioner's birth in the United States.

If the petitioner was born outside the United States and became a citizen through the naturalization or citizenship of a parent or husband and has not been issued a certificate of citizenship in his or her own name, submit evidence of the citizenship and marriage of the parent or husband, as well as termination of any prior marriages. Also, if petitioner claims citizenship through a parent, submit a copy of the petitioner's birth certificate and a separate statement showing the date, place, and means of all his/her arrivals and departures into and out of the United States.

If petitioner's naturalization occurred within 90 days immediately preceding the filing of this petition, or if it occurred prior to September 27, 1906, a copy of the naturalization certificate must accompany the petition.

An unexpired U.S. passport initially issued for ten years may also be submitted.

f of marriage of petitioner and spouse.
married petitioner should submit a copy of certificate of the marriage and proof of ination of all prior marriages of himself or elf and spouse. In the case of an arried petitioner who was previously ied, submit proof of termination of all marriages. **NOTE:** If any change occurs e petitioner's marital status while the is pending, the district director should be ied immediately.

C. A home study with a statement or attachment recommending or approving of the adoption or proposed adoption signed by an official of the responsible state agency in the state of the child's proposed residence or of an agency authorized by that state, or, in the case of a child adopted abroad, of an appropriate public or private adoption agency which is licensed in the United States. Both individuals and organizations may qualify as agencies. If the recommending agency is a licensed agency, the recommendation must set forth that it is licensed, the state in which it is licensed, its license number, if any, and the period of validity of its license. The research, including interviewing, however, and the preparation of the home study may be done by an individual or group in the United States or abroad satisfactory to the recommending agency. A responsible state agency or licensed agency can accept a home study made by an unlicensed or foreign agency and use that home study as a basis for a favorable recommendation. The home study must contain, but is not limited to, the following elements:

(1) the financial ability of the adoptive or prospective parent or parents to rear and educate the child.

(2) a detailed description of the living accommodations where the adoptive or prospective parent or parents currently reside.

(3) A detailed description of the living accommodations where the child will reside.

(4) A factual evaluation of the physical, mental, and moral capabilities of the adoptive or prospective parent or parents in relation to rearing and educating the child.

D. Fingerprints.
Each member of the married prospective adoptive couple or the married prospective adoptive parent, and each additional adult member of the prospective adoptive parents' household must be fingerprinted in connection with this petition.

(1) *Petitioners residing in the United States.* After filing this petition, INS will notify each person in writing of the time and location where they must go to be fingerprinted. Failure to appear to be fingerprinted may result in denial of the petition.

(2) *Petitioners residing Abroad.* Completed fingerprint cards (Forms FD-258)

must be submitted with the petition. Do not bend, fold, or crease completed fingerprint cards. Fingerprint cards must be prepared by a United States consular office or a United States military installation.

3. General Filing Instructions.

A. **Type or print legibly in ink.**

B. **If extra space is needed** to complete any item, attach a continuation sheet, indicate the item number, and date and sign each sheet.

C. **Translations.** Any foreign language document must be accompanied by a full English translation, which the translator has certified as complete and correct, and by the translator's certification that he or she is competent to translate the foreign language into English.

D. **Copies.** If these instructions state that a copy of a document may be filed with this petition and you choose to send us the original, we may keep that original for our records.

4. Submission of Application.
A prospective petitioner residing in the United States should send the completed application to the office of this Service having jurisdiction over his or her place of residence. A prospective petitioner residing outside the United States should consult the nearest American consulate for the overseas or stateside INS office designated to act on the application.

5. Fee. (Read instructions carefully.)
A fee of four hundred and sixty dollars ($460) must be submitted for filing this petition. There is a fifty dollar ($50) per person fingerprinting fee in addition to the petition fee for each person residing in the United States and required to be fingerprinted. For example, if a petition is filed by a married couple residing in the United States with one additional adult member in their household, the total of fees that must be submitted is $610. However, if a petition is filed by a married couple residing abroad, only the petition fee of $460 must be submitted.

One check or money order may be submitted for both the petition fee and the fingerprinting fees. All fees must be submitted in the exact amount. Payment by check or money order must be drawn on a bank or other institution located in the

United States and be payable in United States curr■

If petitioner resides in Guam, the check or money c must be payable to the "Treasurer, Guam."

If petitioner resides in the Virgin Islands, the check money order must be payable to the "Commissione Finance of the Virgin Islands."

All other petitioners must make the check or mone■ order payable to the "Immigration and Naturalizatio■ Service." When a check is drawn on the account c person other than the petitioner, the name of the petitioner must be entered on the face of the chec■

If petition is submitted from outside the United Sta■ remittance may be made by bank international mor■ order or foreign draft drawn on a financial institutic the United States and payable to the Immigration a■ Naturalization Service in United States currency. Personal checks are accepted subject to collectibili■ uncollectible check in payment of a petition fee wi■ render the petition and any document issued invali■ charge of $30.00 will be imposed if a check in pay■ of a fee is not honored by the bank on which it is c

When more than one petition is submitted by the s■ petitioner in behalf of orphans who are siblings, on set of petition and fingerprinting fees is required.

6. When Child/Children Located and/or Identified.
A separate Form I-600, Petition to Classify Orphan Immediate Relative, must be filed for each child. ■ fee is not required if only one form I-600 is filed a■ filed within one year of completion of all advance processing in a case where there has been a favor■ determination concerning the beneficiary orphan.

Normally, Form I-600 should be submitted to the I office where the advance processing application w filed. The immigration and Naturalization Service ■ offices in the following countries: Austria, China, Denmark, Domincan Republic, Ecuador, El Salvadc Germany, Ghana, Great Britain, Greece, Guatemal■ Haiti, Honduras, India, Italy, Jamaica, Kenya, Kore■ Mexico, Pakistan, Panama, Peru, Philippines, Russ■ Singapore, South Africa, Spain, Thailand, and Vie■ A prospective petitioner who is going abroad to ac locate a child in one of these countries should file I-600 at the INS office having jurisdiction over the where the child is residing or will be located, unle■ case is being retained at the stateside office.

However, a prospective petitioner who is going abroad to any other country to adopt or locate a child should file Form I-600 at the American consulate or embassy having jurisdiction over the place where the child is residing or will be located unless the case is being retained at the stateside office.

The case may be retained at the stateside office, if the petitioner requests it and if it appears that the case will be processed more quickly in that manner. Form I-600 must be accompanied by all the evidence required on the instruction sheet of that form, except that the evidence required by and submitted with this form need not be furnished.

Assistance.

Assistance may be obtained from a recognized social agency or from any public or private agency. The following recognized social agencies, which have offices in many of the principal cities of the United States, have agreed to furnish assistance:

Bethany Christian Services.
600 Fivemile Road NE
Grand Rapids, MI. 49525
Tel: (616) 224-7446
Fax: (616) 224-7585

Catholic Legal Immigration Network, Inc. (CLINIC)
415 Michigan Avenue, NE., Suite 150
Washington, DC 20017
Tel: (202) 635-2556
Fax: (202) 632-2649

International Social Services/U.S. of America Branch.
700 Light Street
Baltimore, MD. 21230
Tel: (410) 230-2734
Fax: (410) 230-2741

United States Catholic Conference Migration and Refugee Services (USCC/MRS).
3211 4th Street, NE
Washington, DC 20017
Tel: (202) 541-3352
Fax: (202) 722-8800

8. Penalties.

Willful false statements on this form or supporting documents can be punished by fine or imprisonment. U.S. Code, Title 18, Sec. 1001 (Formerly Sec. 80.)

9. Authority.

8 U.S.C 1154(a). Routine uses for disclosure under the Privacy Act of 1974 have been published in the Federal Register and are available upon request. The Immigration and Naturalization Service will use the information to determine immigrant eligibility. Submission of the information is voluntary, but failure to provide any or all of the information may result in denial of the petition.

10. Reporting Burden.

A person is not required to respond to a collection of information unless it displays a currently valid OMB control number. Public reporting burden for this collection of information is estimated to average 30 minutes per response, including the time for reviewing instructions, searching existing data sources, gathering and maintaining the data needed, and completing and reviewing the collection of information. Send comments regarding this burden estimate or any other aspect of this collection of information, including suggestions for reducing this burden, to: Immigration and Naturalization Service, HQPDI, 425 I Street, N.W., Room 4034, Washington, DC 20536; OMB No. 1115-0049. **DO NOT MAIL YOUR COMPLETED APPLICATION TO THIS ADDRESS.**

Please do not write in this block.

It has been determined that the

☐ Married ☐ Unmarried

Fee Stamp

There

☐ are ☐ are not

preadoptive requirements in the state of the child's proposed residence.

The following is a description of the preadoption requirements, if any, of the state of the child's proposed residence:

DATE OF FAVORABLE DETERMINATION

DD

DISTRICT

The preadoption requirements, if any,

☐ have been met. ☐ have not been met.

File number of petitioner, if applicable

Please type or print legibly in ink.

Application is made by the named prospective petitioner for advance processing of an orphan petition.

BLOCK I - Information about prospective petitioner

1. My name is: (Last)   (First)   (Middle)

2. Other names used (including maiden name if appropriate):

3. I reside in the U.S. at: (C/O if appropriate)   (Apt. No.)

(Number and street)   (Town or city)   (State)   (ZIP Code)

4. Address abroad (if any): (Number and street)   (Apt. No.)

(Town or city)   (Province)   (Country)

5. I was born on: (Month)   (Day)   (Year)

In: (Town or City)   (State or Province)   (Country)

6. My phone number is: (Include Area Code)

7. My marital status is:

☐ Married
☐ Widowed
☐ Divorced
☐ Single

☐ I have never been married.
☐ I have been previously married _____ time(s).

8. If you are now married, give the following information:
Date and place of present marriage

Name of present spouse (include maiden name of wife)

Date of birth of spouse   Place of birth of spouse

Number of prior marriages of spouse

My spouse resides ☐ With me   ☐ Apart from me
(provide address)
(Apt. No.)   (No. and street)   (City)   (State)   (Cou

9. I am a citizen of the United States through:
☐ Birth   ☐ Parents   ☐ Naturalization
If acquired through naturalization, give name under which naturalized, number of naturalization certificate, and date place of naturalization.

If not, submit evidence of citizenship. See Instruction 2.
If acquired through parentage, have you obtained a certif in your own name based on that acquisition?
☐ No   ☐ Yes

Have you or any person through whom you claimed citize ever lost United States citizenship?
☐ No   ☐ Yes (If yes, attach detailed explanat

Continue on reve

Received	Trans. In	Ret'd Trans. Out	Comple

K II - General information

ame and address of organization or individual assisting ou in locating or identifying an orphan

(Name)

_____

(Address)

_____

o you plan to travel abroad to locate or adopt a child?

☐ Yes   ☐ No

oes your spouse, if any, plan to travel abroad to locate or dopt a child?

☐ Yes   ☐ No

the answer to question 11 or 12 is "yes," give the ollowing information:

. Your date of intended departure   _____

. Your spouse's date of intended departure   _____

. City, province   _____

14. Will the child come to the United States for adoption after compliance with the preadoption requirements, if any, of the state of proposed residence?

☐ Yes   ☐ No

15. If the answer to question 14 is "no," will the child be adopted abroad after having been personally seen and observed by you and your spouse, if married?

☐ Yes   ☐ No

16. Where do you wish to file your orphan petition?

The service office located at

_____

The American Embassy or Consulate at

_____

17. Do you plan to adopt more than one child?

☐ Yes   ☐ No

If "Yes", how many children do you plan to adopt?

---

ication of prospective petitioner

ify, under penalty of perjury under the laws of the d States of America, that the foregoing is true and ct and that I will care for an orphan/orphans properly if tted to the United States.

ature of Prospective Petitioner)

uted on (Date)

Certification of married prospective petitioner's spouse

I certify, under penalty of perjury under the laws of the United States of America, that the foregoing is true and correct and that my spouse and I will care for an orphan/orphans properly if admitted to the United States.

(Signature of Prospective Petitioner)

Executed on (Date)

Signature of person preparing form, if other than petitioner

I declare that this document was prepared by me at the request of the prospective petitioner and is based on all information of which I have any knowledge.

(Signature)

Address

Executed on (Date)

INSTRUCTIONS

Purpose of this Form

This form is required to show that an intending immigrant has adequate means of financial support and is not likely to become a public charge.

Sponsor's Obligation

The person completing this affidavit is the sponsor. A sponsor's obligation continues until the sponsored immigrant becomes a U.S. citizen, can be credited with 40 qualifying quarters of work, departs the United States permanently, or dies. Divorce does not terminate the obligation. By signing this form, you, the sponsor, agree to support the intending immigrant and any spouse and/or children immigrating with him or her and to reimburse any government agency or private entity that provides these sponsored immigrants with Federal, State, or local means-tested public benefits.

General Filing Instructions

Please answer all questions by typing or clearly printing in black ink only. Indicate that an item is not applicable with "N/A". If an answer is "none," please so state. If you need extra space to answer any item, attach a sheet of paper with your name and Social Security number, and indicate the number of the item to which the answer refers.

You must submit an affidavit of support for each applicant for immigrant status. You may submit photocopies of this affidavit for any spouse or children immigrating with an immigrant you are sponsoring. For purposes of this form, a spouse or child is immigrating with an immigrant you are sponsoring if he or she is: 1) listed in Part 3 of this affidavit of support; and 2) applies for an immigrant visa or adjustment of status within 6 months of the date this affidavit of support is originally completed and signed. The signature on the affidavit must be notarized by a notary public or signed before an Immigration or a Consular officer.

You should give the completed affidavit of support with all required documentation to the sponsored immigrant for submission to either a Consular Officer with Form OF-230, Application for Immigrant Visa and Alien Registration, or an Immigration Officer with Form I-485, Application to Register Permanent Residence or Adjust Status. You may enclose the affidavit of support and accompanying documents in a sealed envelope to be opened only by the designated Government official. The sponsored immigrant must submit the affidavit of support to the Government within 6 months of its signature.

Who Needs an Affidavit of Support under Section 213A?

This affidavit must be filed at the time an intending immigrant is applying for an immigrant visa or adjustment of status. It is required for:

- All immediate relatives, including orphans, and family-based immigrants. (Self-petitioning widow/er and battered spouses and children are exempt from t■ requirement); and

- Employment-based immigrants where a relative filed immigrant visa petition or has a significant ownershi■ interest (5 percent or more) in the entity that filed the petition.

Who Completes an Affidavit of Support under Section 213■

- For immediate relatives and family-based immigrants family member petitioning for the intending immigra■ must be the sponsor.

- For employment-based immigrants, the petitioning relative or a relative with a significant ownership inte■ (5 percent or more) in the petitioning entity must be ■ sponsor. The term "relative," for these purposes, is defined as husband, wife, father, mother, child, adult or daughter, brother, or sister.

- If the petitioner cannot meet the income requirement■ joint sponsor may submit an additional affidavit of support.

A sponsor, or joint sponsor, must also be:

- A citizen or national of the United States or an alien lawfully admitted to the United States for permanent residence;

- At least 18 years of age; and

- Domiciled in the United States or its territories and possessions.

Sponsor's Income Requirement

As a sponsor, your household income must equal or exceed ■ percent of the Federal poverty line for your household size. F the purpose of the affidavit of support, household size include yourself, all persons related to you by birth, marriage, or adoption living in your residence, your dependents, any immigrants you have previously sponsored using INS Form I-864 if that obligation has not terminated, and the intending immigrant(s) in Part 3 of this affidavit of support. The pover■ guidelines are calculated and published annually by the Department of Health and Human Services. Sponsors who ar■ on active duty in the U.S. Armed Forces other than for trainir■ need only demonstrate income at 100 percent of the poverty line *if* they are submitting this affidavit for the purpose of sponsoring their spouse or child.

If you are currently employed and have an *individual* income which meets or exceeds 125 percent of the Federal poverty li■ or (100 percent, if applicable) for your household size, you d■ not need to list the income of any other person. When determining your income, you may include the income gener■ by individuals related to you by birth, marriage, or

n who are living in your residence, if they have lived in
sidence for the previous 6 months, or who are listed as
ents on your most recent Federal income tax return
r or not they live in your residence. For their income to
idered, these household members or dependents must be
to make their income available for the support of the
ed immigrant(s) if necessary, and to complete and sign
864A, Contract Between Sponsor and Household
r. However, a household member who is the immigrant
sponsoring only need complete Form I-864A if his or her
will be used to determine your ability to support a
and/or children immigrating with him or her.

y of the most recent 3 tax years, you and your spouse
ported income on a joint income tax return, but you want
nly your own income to qualify (and your spouse is not
ing a Form I-864A), you may provide a separate breakout
individual income for these years. Your individual
will be based on the earnings from your W-2 forms,
nd Tax Statement, submitted to IRS for any such years.
ssary to meet the income requirement, you may also
evidence of other income listed on your tax returns
can be attributed to you. You must provide
entation of such reported income, including Forms 1099
the payer, which show your name and Social Security
r.

ust calculate your household size and total household
as indicated in Parts 4.B. and 4.C. of this form. You must
re your total household income with the minimum income
ment for your household size using the poverty
nes. For the purposes of the affidavit of support,
ination of your ability to meet the income requirements
based on the most recent poverty guidelines published
ederal Register at the time the Consular or Immigration
r makes a decision on the intending immigrant's
tion for an immigrant visa or adjustment of status.
ration and Consular Officers will begin to use updated
y guidelines on the first day of the second month after
e the guidelines are published in the Federal Register.

total household income is equal to or higher than the
m income requirement for your household size, you do
d to provide information on your assets, and you may
e a joint sponsor unless you are requested to do so by a
ar or Immigration Officer. If your total household income
t meet the minimum income requirement, the intending
ant will be ineligible for an immigrant visa or adjustment of
unless:

You provide evidence of assets that meet the
requirements outlined under "Evidence of Assets"
below; and/or

The immigrant you are sponsoring provides evidence
of assets that meet the requirements under "Evidence of
Assets" below; or

A joint sponsor assumes the liability of the intending
immigrant with you. A joint sponsor must execute a
separate affidavit of support on behalf of the intending

immigrant and any accompanying family members. A
joint sponsor must individually meet the minimum
requirement of 125 percent of the poverty line based on
his or her household size and income and/or assets,
including any assets of the sponsored immigrant.

The Government may pursue verification of any information
provided on or in support of this form, including employment,
income, or assets with the employer, financial or other
institutions, the Internal Revenue Service, or the Social Security
Administration.

Evidence of Income

In order to complete this form you must submit the following
evidence of income:

- A copy of your complete Federal income tax return, as
  filed with the Internal Revenue Service, for each of the
  most recent 3 tax years. If you were not required to file a
  tax return in any of the most recent 3 tax years, you must
  provide an explanation. If you filed a joint income tax
  return and are using only your own income to qualify,
  you must also submit copies of your W-2s for each of
  the most recent 3 tax years, and if necessary to meet the
  income requirement, evidence of other income reported
  on your tax returns, such as Forms 1099.

- If you rely on income of any members of your
  household or dependents in order to reach the minimum
  income requirement, copies of their Federal income tax
  returns for the most recent 3 tax years. These persons
  must each complete and sign a Form I-864A, Contract
  Between Sponsor and Household Member.

- Evidence of current employment or self-employment,
  such as a recent pay statement, or a statement from your
  employer on business stationery, showing beginning
  date of employment, type of work performed, and salary
  or wages paid. You must also provide evidence of
  current employment for any person whose income is
  used to qualify.

Evidence of Assets

If you want to use your assets, the assets of your household
members or dependents, and/or the assets of the immigrant you
are sponsoring to meet the minimum income requirement, you
must provide evidence of assets with a cash value that equals at
least five times the difference between your total household
income and the minimum income requirement. For the assets of
a household member, other than the immigrant(s) you are
sponsoring, to be considered, the household member must
complete and sign Form I-864A, Contract Between Sponsor and
Household Member.

All assets must be supported with evidence to verify location,
ownership, and value of each asset. Any liens and liabilities
relating to the assets must be documented. List only assets that
can be readily converted into cash within one year. Evidence of
assets includes, but is not limited to the following:

- Bank statements covering the last 12 months, *or a* statement from an officer of the bank or other financial institution in which you have deposits, including deposit/withdrawal history for the last 12 months, and current balance;

- Evidence of ownership and value of stocks, bonds, and certificates of deposit, and date(s) acquired;

- Evidence of ownership and value of other personal property, and date(s) acquired; and

- Evidence of ownership and value of any real estate, and date(s) acquired.

Change of Sponsor's Address

You are required by 8 U.S.C. 1183a(d) and 8 CFR 213a.3 to report every change of address to the Immigration and Naturalization Service and the State(s) in which the sponsored immigrant(s) reside(s). You must report changes of address to INS on Form I-865, Sponsor's Notice of Change of Address, within 30 days of any change of address. You must also report any change in your address to the State(s) in which the sponsored immigrant(s) live.

Penalties

If you include in this affidavit of support any material information that you know to be false, you may be liable for criminal prosecution under the laws of the United States.

If you fail to give notice of your change of address, as required by 8 U.S.C. 1183a(d) and 8 CFR 213a.3, you may be liable for the civil penalty established by 8 U.S.C. 1183a(d)(2). The amount of the civil penalty will depend on whether you failed to give this notice because you were aware that the immigrant(s) you sponsored had received Federal, State, or local means-tested public benefits.

Privacy Act Notice

Authority for the collection of the information requested on this form is contained in 8 U.S.C. 1182(a)(4), 1183a, 1184(a), and 1258. The information will be used principally by the INS or by any Consular Officer to whom it is furnished, to support an alien's application for benefits under the Immigration and Nationality Act and specifically the assertion that he or she has adequate means of financial support and will not become a public charge. Submission of the information is voluntary. Failure to provide the information will result in denial of the application for an immigrant visa or adjustment of status.

The information may also, as a matter of routine use, be disclosed to other Federal, State, and local agencies or private entities providing means-tested public benefits for use in civil action against the sponsor for breach of contract. It may also be disclosed as a matter of routine use to other Federal, State, local, and foreign law enforcement and regulatory agencies to enable these entities to carry out their law enforcement responsibilites.

Reporting Burden

A person is not required to respond to a collection of information unless it displays a currently valid OMB control number. We try to create forms and instructions that are accurate, can be easily understood, and which impose the least possible burden on you to provide us with information. Often it is difficult because some immigration laws are very complex. reporting burden for this collection of information on Form I-86 computed as follows: 1) learning about the form, 63 minutes; 2 completing the form, 105 minutes; and 3) assembling and filin, form, 65 minutes, for an estimated average of 3 hours and 48 minutes minutes per response. The reporting burden for collect of information on Form I-864A is computed as: 1) learning abo the form, 20 minutes; 2) completing the form, 55 minutes; 3) assembling and filing the form, 30 minutes, for an estimated average of 1 hour and 45 minutes per response. If you have comments regarding the accuracy of this estimates, or suggestions for making this form simpler, you can write to the Immigration and Naturalization Service, HQPDI, 425 I Street, Room 4034, Washington, DC 20536. **DO NOT MAIL YOUR COMPLETED AFFIDAVIT OF SUPPORT TO THIS ADI**

CHECK LIST

The following items must be submitted with Form I-864, A of Support Under Section 213A:

For *ALL* sponsors:

☐ This form, the **I-864, completed and signed** before public or a Consular or Immigration Officer.

☐ Proof of **current employment** or self employment.

☐ Your individual Federal **income tax returns for th recent 3 tax years,** or an explanation if fewer are submitted. Your **W-2s** for any of the most recent 3 years for which you filed a joint tax return but are us only your own income to qualify. Forms 1099 or ev of other reported income *if* necessary to qualify.

For *SOME* sponsors:

☐ *If the immigrant you are sponsoring is bringing a or children,* **photocopies of the immigrant's affid support** for each spouse and/or child immigrating w immigrant you are sponsoring.

☐ *If you are on active duty in the U.S. Armed Forces sponsoring a spouse or child using the 100 percen poverty level exception,* **proof of your active milit status.**

If you are using the income of persons in your hous dependents to qualify,

☐ A separate **Form I-864A** for each person w income you will use. A sponsored immigrant/household member who is not immigrating with a spouse and/or child **does need to complete Form I-864A.**

☐ Proof of their **residency and relationship t** if they are not listed as dependents on your income tax return for the most recent tax yea

☐ Proof of their **current employment** or self-employment.

]   Copies of their individual Federal **income tax returns for the 3 most recent tax years,** or an explanation if fewer are submitted.

If you use your assets or the assets of the sponsored immigrant to qualify,

]   **Documentation of assets** establishing location, ownership, date of acquisition, and value. Evidence of any liens or liabilities against these assets.

]   A separate **Form I-864A** for each household member other than the sponsored immigrant/household member.

If you are a joint sponsor or the relative of an employment-based immigrant requiring an affidavit of support, **proof of your citizenship status.**

]   For U.S. citizens or nationals, a copy of your birth certificate, passport, or certificate of naturalization or citizenship.

]   For lawful permanent residents, a copy of both sides of your I-551, Permanent Resident Card.

OMB No.

U.S. Department of Justice
Immigration and Naturalization Service

Affidavit of Support Under S
213A of the Act

START HERE - Please Type or Print

Part 1. Information on Sponsor (You)

Last Name	First Name	Middle Name

Mailing Address *(Street Number and Name)*	Apt/Suite Number

City	State or Province

Country	ZIP/Postal Code	Telephone N

Place of Residence if different from above *(Street Number and Name)* Apt/Suite Number

City	State or Province

Country	ZIP/Postal Code	Telephone Number

Date of Birth *(Month, Day, Year)*	Place of Birth *(City, State, Country)*	Are you a U.S. Citizen? ☐ Yes ☐ No

Social Security Number	A-Number *(If any)*

FOR AGENCY USE O

This Affidavit   Recei

[ ] Meets

[ ] Does not
meet

Requirements of
Section 213A

Part 2. Basis for Filing Affidavit of Support

I am filing this affidavit of support because *(check one):*

a. ☐ I filed/am filing the alien relative petition.

b. ☐ I filed/am filing an alien worker petition on behalf of the intending

immigrant, who is related to me as my _____ .
(relationship)

c. ☐ I have ownership interest of at least 5% _____ .
(name of entity which filed visa petition)

which filed an alien worker petition on behalf of the intending

immigrant, who is related to me as my _____ .
(relationship)

d. ☐ I am a joint sponsor willing to accept the legal obligations with any other sponsor(s).

Officer or I.J.
Signature

Location

Date

Part 3. Information on the Immigrant(s) You Are Sponsoring

Last Name	First Name	Middle Name

Date of Birth *(Month,Day, Year)*	Sex ☐ Male ☐ Female	Social Security Number *(If any)*

Country of Citizenship	A-Number *(If any)*

Current Address *(Street Number and Name)*	Apt/Suite Number	City

State/Province	Country	ZIP/Postal Code	Telephone Number

List any spouse and/or children immigrating with the immigrant named above in this Part: *(Use additional sheet of paper if necessc*

Name	Relationship to Sponsored Immigrant			Date of Birth			A-Number *(If any)*	Social Sec *(If any*
	Spouse	Son	Daughter	Mo.	Day	Yr.		

Form I-864 (Rev. 11

a sponsor you must be a U.S. citizen or national or a lawful permanent resident. If you are not the petitioning relative, you ...rovide proof of status. To prove status, U.S. citizens or nationals must attach a copy of a document proving status, such as passport, birth certificate, or certificate of naturalization, and lawful permanent residents must attach a copy of both sides of ...ermanent Resident Card (Form I-551).

...termination of your eligibility to sponsor an immigrant will be based on an evaluation of your demonstrated ability to ...in an annual income at or above 125 percent of the Federal poverty line (100 percent if you are a petitioner sponsoring your ... or child and you are on active duty in the U.S. Armed Forces). The assessment of your ability to maintain an adequate ...e will include your current employment, household size, and household income as shown on the Federal income tax returns ... 3 most recent tax years. Assets that are readily converted to cash and that can be made available for the support of ...red immigrants if necessary, including any such assets of the immigrant(s) you are sponsoring, may also be considered.

...eatest weight in determining eligibility will be placed on current employment and household income. If a petitioner is unable ...onstrate ability to meet the stated income and asset requirements, a joint sponsor who *can* meet the income and asset ...ments is needed. Failure to provide adequate evidence of income and/or assets or an affidavit of support completed by a ...ponsor will result in denial of the immigrant's application for an immigrant visa or adjustment to permanent resident status.

...onsor's Employment

1. ☐ Employed by _____ *(Provide evidence of employment)*

   Annual salary _____ or hourly wage $ _____ *(for _____ hours per week)*

2. ☐ Self employed _____ *(Name of business)*

   Nature of employment or business _____

3. ☐ Unemployed or retired since _____

...onsor's Household Size   Number

...mber of persons (related to you by birth, marriage, or adoption) living in your residence, including ...urself *(Do NOT include persons being sponsored in this affidavit.)* _____

...mber of immigrants being sponsored in this affidavit *(Include all persons in Part 3.)* _____

...mber of immigrants **NOT** living in your household whom you are obligated to support under a ...eviously signed Form I-864. _____

...mber of persons who are otherwise dependent on you, as claimed in your tax return for the most ...cent tax year. _____

...tal household size. *(Add lines 1 through 4.)*   **Total** _____

...ersons below who are included in lines 1 or 3 for whom you previously have submitted INS Form I-864, *if your support ...ation has not terminated.*

...ditional space is needed, use additional paper)

Name	A-Number	Date Affidavit of Support Signed	Relationship

Part 4.   Eligibility to Sponsor   *(Continued)*

C. Sponsor's Annual Household Income

Enter total unadjusted income from your Federal income tax return for the most recent tax year below. If you last filed a joint income tax return but are using only your *own* income to qualify, list total earnings from your W-2 Forms, or, *if* necessary to reach the required income for your household size, include income from other sources listed on your tax return. If your *individual* income does not meet the income requirement for your household size, you may also list total income for anyone related to you by birth, marriage, or adoption currently living with you in your residence if they have lived in your residence for the previous 6 months, or any person shown as a dependent on your Federal income tax return for the most recent tax year, even if not living in the household. For their income to be considered, household members or dependents must be willing to make their income available for support of the sponsored immigrant(s) and to complete and sign Form I-864A, Contract Between Sponsor and Household Member. A sponsored immigrant/household member only need complete Form I-864A if his or her income will be used to determin your ability to support a spouse and/or children immigrating with him or her.

You must attach evidence of current employment and copies of income tax returns as filed with the IRS for the most recent 3 tax years for yourself and all persons whose income is listed below. See "Required Evidence " in Instructions. Income from all 3 ye will be considered in determining your ability to support the immigrant(s) you are sponsoring.

☐ I filed a single/separate tax return for the most recent tax year.

☐ I filed a joint return for the most recent tax year which includes only my own income.

☐ I filed a joint return for the most recent tax year which includes income for my spouse and myself.

    ☐ I am submitting documentation of my individual income (Forms W-2 and 1099).

    ☐ I am qualifying using my spouse's income; my spouse is submitting a Form I-864A.

Indicate most recent tax year
_____
(tax year)

Sponsor's individual income $ _____

or

Sponsor and spouse's combined income $ _____
(If spouse's income is to be considered, spouse must submit Form I-864A.)

Income of other qualifying persons.
(List names; include spouse if applicable. Each person must complete Form I-864A.)

_____ $ _____

_____ $ _____

_____ $ _____

Total Household Income $ _____

Explain on separate sheet of paper if you or any of the above listed individuals were not required to file Federal income tax returns for the most recent 3 years, or if other explanation of income, employment, or evidence is necessary.

D. Determination of Eligibility Based on Income

1.   ☐ I am subject to the 125 percent of poverty line requirement for sponsors.
     ☐ I am subject to the 100 percent of poverty line requirement for sponsors on active duty in the U.S. Armed Forces sponsoring their spouse or child.

2.   Sponsor's total household size, from Part 4.B., line 5   _____ .

3.   Minimum income requirement from the Poverty Guidelines chart for the year of   _____ is $ _____
    for this household size.   *(year)*

If you are currently employed and your household income for your household size is equal to or greater than the applicable poverty line requirement (from line D.3.), you do not need to list assets (Parts 4.E. and 5) or have a joint sponsor (Part 6) unl you are requested to do so by a Consular or Immigration Officer. You may skip to Part 7, Use of the Affidavit of Support to Overcome Public Charge Ground of Admissibility. **Otherwise, you should continue with Part 4.E.**

rt 4. Eligibility to Sponsor *(Continued)*

Sponsor's Assets and Liabilities

ur assets and those of your qualifying household members and dependents may be used to demonstrate ability to maintain an ome at or above 125 percent (or 100 percent, if applicable) of the poverty line *if* they are available for the support of the sponsored nigrant(s) and can readily be converted into cash within 1 year. The household member, other than the immigrant(s) you are ¬nsoring, must complete and sign Form I-864A, Contract Between Sponsor and Household Member. List the cash value of each et *after* any debts or liens are subtracted. Supporting evidence must be attached to establish location, ownership, date of ¬uisition, and value of each asset listed, including any liens and liabilities related to each asset listed. See "Evidence of Assets" in tructions.

Type of Asset	Cash Value of Assets *(Subtract any debts)*
Savings deposits	$
Stocks, bonds, certificates of deposit	$
Life insurance cash value	$
Real estate	$
Other *(specify)*	$
Total Cash Value of Assets	$ _____

rt 5. Immigrant's Assets and Offsetting Liabilities

sponsored immigrant's assets may also be used in support of your ability to maintain income at or above 125 percent of the erty line *if* the assets are or will be available in the United States for the support of the sponsored immigrant(s) and can readily onverted into cash within 1 year.

sponsored immigrant should provide information on his or her assets in a format similar to part 4.E. above. Supporting evidence t be attached to establish location, ownership, and value of each asset listed, including any liens and liabilities for each asset d. See "Evidence of Assets" in Instructions.

t 6. Joint Sponsors

¬usehold income and assets do not meet the appropriate poverty line for your household size, a joint sponsor is required. There be more than one joint sponsor, but each joint sponsor must individually meet the 125 percent of poverty line requirement d on his or her household income and/or assets, including any assets of the sponsored immigrant. By submitting a separate lavit of Support under Section 213A of the Act (Form I-864), a joint sponsor accepts joint responsibility with the petitioner for ponsored immigrant(s) until they become U.S. citizens, can be credited with 40 quarters of work, leave the United States anently, or die.

t 7. Use of the Affidavit of Support to Overcome Public Charge Ground of Inadmissibility

on 212(a)(4)(C) of the Immigration and Nationality Act provides that an alien seeking permanent residence as an immediate ¬ve (including an orphan), as a family-sponsored immigrant, or as an alien who will accompany or follow to join another alien is dered to be likely to become a public charge and is inadmissible to the United States unless a sponsor submits a legally ¬ceable affidavit of support on behalf of the alien. Section 212(a)(4)(D) imposes the same requirement on an employment-based grant, and those aliens who accompany or follow to join the employment- based immigrant, if the employment-based immigrant ¬e employed by a relative, or by a firm in which a relative owns a significant interest. Separate affidavits of support are required mily members at the time they immigrate if they are not included on this affidavit of support or do not apply for an immigrant ¬r adjustment of status within 6 months of the date this affidavit of support is originally signed. The sponsor must provide the ¬ored immigrant(s) whatever support is necessary to maintain them at an income that is at least 125 percent of the Federal ty guidelines.

I submit this affidavit of support in consideration of the sponsored immigrant(s) not being found inadmissible to the United States under section 212(a)(4)(C) (or 212(a)(4)(D) for an employment-based immigrant) and to enable the sponsored immigrant(s) to overcome this ground of inadmissibility. I agree to provide the sponsored immigrant(s) whatever support is necessary to maintain the sponsored immigrant(s) at an income that is at least 125 percent of the Federal poverty guidelines. I understand that my obligation will continue until my death or the sponsored immigrant(s) have become U.S. citizens, can be credited with 40 quarters of work, depart the United States permanently, or die.

Notice of Change of Address.

Sponsors are required to provide written notice of any change of address within 30 days of the change in address until the sponsored immigrant(s) have become U.S. citizens, can be credited with 40 quarters of work, depart the United States permanently, or die. To comply with this requirement, the sponsor must complete INS Form I-865. Failure to give this notice may subject the sponsor to the civil penalty established under section 213A(d)(2) which ranges from $250 to $2,000, unless the failure to report occurred with the knowledge that the sponsored immigrant(s) had received means-tested public benefits, in which case the penalty ranges from $2,000 to $5,000.

> *If my address changes for any reason before my obligations under this affidavit of support terminate, I will complete and file INS Form I-865, Sponsor's Notice of Change of Address, within 30 days of the change of address. I understand that failure to give this notice may subject me to civil penalties.*

Means-tested Public Benefit Prohibitions and Exceptions.

Under section 403(a) of Public Law 104-193 (Welfare Reform Act), aliens lawfully admitted for permanent residence in the United States, with certain exceptions, are ineligible for most Federally-funded means-tested public benefits during their first 5 years in the United States. This provision does not apply to public benefits specified in section 403(c) of the Welfare Reform Act or to State public benefits, including emergency Medicaid; short-term, non-cash emergency relief; services provided under the National School Lunch and Child Nutrition Acts; immunizations and testing and treatment for communicable diseases; student assistance under the Higher Education Act and the Public Health Service Act; certain forms of foster-care or adoption assistance under the Social Security Act; Head Start programs; means-tested programs under the Elementary and Secondary Education Act; and Job Training Partnership Act programs.

Consideration of Sponsor's Income in Determining Eligibility for Benefits.

If a permanent resident alien is no longer statutorily barred from a Federally-funded means-tested public benefit program and applies for such a benefit, the income and resources of the sponsor and the sponsor's spouse will be considered (or deemed) to be the income and resources of the sponsored immigrant in determining the immigrant's eligibility for Federal means-tested public benefits. Any State or local government may also choose to consider (or deem) the income and resources of the sponsor and the sponsor's spouse to be the income and resources of the immigrant for the purposes of determining eligibility for their means-tested public benefits. The attribution of the income and resources of the sponsor and the sponsor's spouse to the immigrant will continue until the immigrant becomes a U.S. citizen or has worked or can be credited with 40 qualifying quarters of work, provided that the immigrant or the worker crediting the quarters to the immigrant has not received any Federal means-tested public benefit during any creditable quarter for any period after December 31, 1996.

> *I understand that, under section 213A of the Immigration and Nationality Act (the Act), as amended, this affidavit of support constitutes a contract between me and the U.S. Government. This contract is designed to protect the United States Government, and State and local government agencies or private entities that provide means-tested public benefits, from having to pay benefits to or on behalf of the sponsored immigrant(s), for as long as I am obligated to support them under this affidavit of support. I understand that the sponsored immigrants, or any Federal, State, local, or private entity that pays any means-tested benefit to or on behalf of the sponsored immigrant(s), are entitled to sue me if I fail to meet my obligations under this affidavit of support, as defined by section 213A and INS regulations.*

Civil Action to Enforce.

If the immigrant on whose behalf this affidavit of support is executed receives any Federal, State, or local means-tested public benefit before this obligation terminates, the Federal, State, or local agency or private entity may request reimbursement from the sponsor who signed this affidavit. If the sponsor fails to honor the request for reimbursement, the agency may sue the sponsor in any U.S. District Court or any State court with jurisdiction of civil actions for breach of contract. INS will provide names, addresses and Social Security account numbers of sponsors to benefit-providing agencies for this purpose. Sponsors may also be liable for paying the costs of collection, including legal fees.

7. Use of the Affidavit of Support to Overcome Public Charge Grounds *(Continued)*

I acknowledge that section 213A(a)(1)(B) of the Act grants the sponsored immigrant(s) and any Federal, State, local, or private agency that pays any means-tested public benefit to or on behalf of the sponsored immigrant(s) standing to sue me for failing to meet my obligations under this affidavit of support. I agree to submit to the personal jurisdiction of any court of the United States or of any State, territory, or possession of the United States if the court has subject matter jurisdiction of a civil lawsuit to enforce this affidavit of support. I agree that no lawsuit to enforce this affidavit of support shall be barred by any statute of limitations that might otherwise apply, so long as the plaintiff initiates the civil lawsuit no later than ten (10) years after the date on which a sponsored immigrant last received any means-tested public benefits.

Collection of Judgment.

I acknowledge that a plaintiff may seek specific performance of my support obligation. Furthermore, any money judgment against me based on this affidavit of support may be collected through the use of a judgment lien under 28 U.S.C 3201, a writ of execution under 28 U.S.C 3203, a judicial installment payment order under 28 U.S.C 3204, garnishment under 28 U.S.C 3205, or through the use of any corresponding remedy under State law. I may also be held liable for costs of collection, including attorney fees.

Concluding Provisions.

I, _____, *certify under penalty of perjury under the laws of the United States that:*

    (a) I know the contents of this affidavit of support signed by me;

    (b) All the statements in this affidavit of support are true and correct,

    (c) I make this affidavit of support for the consideration stated in Part 7, freely, and without any mental reservation or purpose of evasion;

    (d) Income tax returns submitted in support of this affidavit are true copies of the returns filed with the Internal Revenue Service; and

    (e) Any other evidence submitted is true and correct.

_____   _____
(Sponsor's Signature)   *(Date)*

Subscribed and sworn to (or affirmed) before me this

_____ day of _____, _____
                 (Month)   *(Year)*

commission expires on _____.

_____
(Signature of Notary Public or Officer Administering Oath)

_____
(Title)

8. If someone other than the sponsor prepared this affidavit of support, that person must complete the following:

I certify under penalty of perjury under the laws of the United States that I prepared this affidavit of support at the sponsor's request, and that this affidavit of support is based on all information of which I have knowledge.

...ure	Print Your Name	Date	Daytime Telephone Number
...ame and Address			

Index

About the Author

Brette McWhorter Sember received her J.D. from the State University of New York at Buffalo. She practiced law in New York state and was a member of the Surrogate's Court committee of the Bar Association of Erie County and was on the Guardian ad litem panel in two counties. Her practice included estate planning and probate.

Sember is experienced in helping seniors sort through options and evaluate choices that involve lifestyle, care facilities, finances and estate and health planning. Her one to one experience with seniors gave her understanding about the deeply personal nature of senior planning and also developed her belief that senior planning is an issue for the entire family. Additionally, her own family experience with aging grandparents makes senior care a day to day issue.

Sember is the author of several self-help legal guides that deal with family and financial issues. She writes and speaks often about law.

Visit her web site at **www.MooseintheBirdbath.com.**

SPHINX® PUBLISHING ORDER FORM

ISBN	Title	Retail	Qty	ISBN	Title	Retail
	SPHINX PUBLISHING NATIONAL TITLES		___	1-57248-158-7	Incorporate in Nevada from Any State	$24.95
_ 1-57248-363-6	101 Complaint Letters That Get Results	$18.95	___	1-57248-250-8	Inmigración a los EE.UU. Paso a Paso	$22.95
_ 1-57248-361-X	The 529 College Savings Plan (2E)	$18.95	___	1-57248-400-4	Inmigración y Ciudadania en los EE. UU.	$16.95
_ 1-57248-349-0	The Antique and Art Collector's Legal Guide	$24.95			Preguntas y Respuestas	
_ 1-57248-347-4	Attorney Responsibilities & Client Rights	$19.95	___	1-57248-377-6	The Law (In Plain English)® for Small Business	$19.95
_ 1-57248-148-X	Cómo Hacer su Propio Testamento	$16.95	___	1-57248-374-1	Law School 101	$16.95
_ 1-57248-226-5	Cómo Restablecer su propio Crédito y	$21.95	___	1-57248-223-0	Legal Research Made Easy (3E)	$21.95
_	Renegociar sus Deudas		___	1-57248-165-X	Living Trusts and Other Ways to	$24.95
_ 1-57248-147-1	Cómo Solicitar su Propio Divorcio	$24.95			Avoid Probate (3E)	
_ 1-57248-166-8	The Complete Book of Corporate Forms	$24.95	___	1-57248-186-2	Manual de Beneficios para el Seguro Social	$18.95
_ 1-57248-353-9	The Complete Kit to Selling Your Own Home	$18.95	___	1-57248-220-6	Mastering the MBE	$16.95
_ 1-57248-229-X	The Complete Legal Guide to Senior Care	$21.95	___	1-57248-167-6	Most Val. Business Legal Forms	$21.95
_ 1-57248-391-1	The Complete Partnership Book	$24.95			You'll Ever Need (3E)	
_ 1-57248-201-X	The Complete Patent Book	$26.95	___	1-57248-360-1	Most Val. Personal Legal Forms	$26.95
_ 1-57248-369-5	Credit Smart	$18.95			You'll Ever Need (2E)	
_ 1-57248-163-3	Crime Victim's Guide to Justice (2E)	$21.95	___	1-57248-388-1	The Power of Attorney Handbook (5E)	$22.95
_ 1-57248-367-9	Employees' Rights	$18.95	___	1-57248-332-6	Profit from Intellectual Property	$28.95
_ 1-57248-365-2	Employer's Rights	$24.95	___	1-57248-329-6	Protect Your Patent	$24.95
_ 1-57248-251-6	The Entrepreneur's Internet Handbook	$21.95	___	1-57248-385-7	Quick Cash	$14.95
_ 1-57248-235-4	The Entrepreneur's Legal Guide	$26.95	___	1-57248-344-X	Repair Your Own Credit and Deal with Debt (2E)	$18.95
_ 1-57248-346-6	Essential Guide to Real Estate Contracts (2E)	$18.95	___	1-57248-350-4	El Seguro Social Preguntas y Respuestas	$16.95
_ 1-57248-160-9	Essential Guide to Real Estate Leases	$18.95	___	1-57248-217-6	Sexual Harassment: Your Guide to Legal Action	$18.95
_ 1-57248-254-0	Family Limited Partnership	$26.95	___	1-57248-219-2	The Small Business Owner's Guide to Bankruptcy	$21.95
_ 1-57248-331-8	Gay & Lesbian Rights	$26.95	___	1-57248-168-4	The Social Security Benefits Handbook (3E)	$18.95
_ 1-57248-139-0	Grandparents' Rights (3E)	$24.95	___	1-57248-216-8	Social Security Q&A	$12.95
_ 1-57248-188-9	Guía de Inmigración a Estados Unidos (3E)	$24.95	___	1-57248-221-4	Teen RIghts	$22.95
_ 1-57248-187-0	Guía de Justicia para Victimas del Crimen	$21.95	___	1-57248-366-0	Tax Smarts for Small Business	$21.95
_ 1-57248-253-2	Guía Esencial para los Contratos de	$22.95	___	1-57248-335-0	Traveler's Rights	$21.95
	Arrendamiento de Bienes Raices		___	1-57248-236-2	Unmarried Parents' Rights (2E)	$19.95
1-57248-103-X	Help Your Lawyer Win Your Case (2E)	$14.95	___	1-57248-362-8	U.S. Immigration and Citizenship Q&A	$18.95
1-57248-334-2	Homeowner's Rights	$19.95	___	1-57248-387-3	U.S. Immigration Step by Step (2E)	$24.95
1-57248-164-1	How to Buy a Condominium or Townhome (2E)	$19.95	___	1-57248-392-X	U.S.A. Immigration Guide (5E)	$26.95
1-57248-328-8	How to Buy Your First Home	$18.95	___	1-57248-192-7	The Visitation Handbook	$18.95
1-57248-191-9	How to File Your Own Bankruptcy (5E)	$21.95	___	1-57248-225-7	Win Your Unemployment	$21.95
1-57248-343-1	How to File Your Own Divorce (5E)	$26.95			Compensation Claim (2E)	
1-57248-222-2	How to Form a Limited Liability Company (2E)	$24.95	___	1-57248-330-X	The Wills, Estate Planning and Trusts Legal Kit	&26.95
1-57248-231-1	How to Form a Nonprofit Corporation (2E)	$24.95	___	1-57248-138-2	Winning Your Personal Injury Claim (2E)	$24.95
1-57248-345-8	How to Form Your Own Corporation (4E)	$26.95	___	1-57248-333-4	Working with Your Homeowners Association	$19.95
1-57248-232-X	How to Make Your Own Simple Will (3E)	$18.95	___	1-57248-380-6	Your Right to Child Custody,	$24.95
1-57248-379-2	How to Register Your Own Copyright (5E)	$24.95			Visitation and Support (3E)	
1-57248-104-8	How to Register Your Own Trademark (3E)	$21.95				
1-57248-394-6	How to Write Your Own Living Will (4E)	$18.95		**Form Continued on Following Page**	**SubTotal** ___	
1-57248-156-0	How to Write Your Own	$24.95				
	Premarital Agreement (3E)					
1-57248-230-3	Incorporate in Delaware from Any State	$26.95				

Qty	ISBN	Title	Retail
		CALIFORNIA TITLES	
____	1-57248-150-1	CA Power of Attorney Handbook (2E)	$18.95
____	1-57248-337-7	How to File for Divorce in CA (4E)	$26.95
____	1-57248-145-5	How to Probate and Settle an Estate in CA	$26.95
____	1-57248-336-9	How to Start a Business in CA (2E)	$21.95
____	1-57248-194-3	How to Win in Small Claims Court in CA (2E)	$18.95
____	1-57248-246-X	Make Your Own CA Will	$18.95
____	1-57248-397-0	The Landlord's Legal Guide in CA (2E)	$24.95
____	1-57248-241-9	Tenants' Rights in CA	$21.95
		FLORIDA TITLES	
____	1-57071-363-4	Florida Power of Attorney Handbook (2E)	$16.95
____	1-57248-396-2	How to File for Divorce in FL (8E)	$28.95
____	1-57248-356-3	How to Form a Corporation in FL (6E)	$24.95
____	1-57248-203-6	How to Form a Limited Liability Co. in FL (2E)	$24.95
____	1-57071-401-0	How to Form a Partnership in FL	$22.95
____	1-57248-113-7	How to Make a FL Will (6E)	$16.95
____	1-57248-088-2	How to Modify Your FL Divorce Judgment (4E)	$24.95
____	1-57248-354-7	How to Probate and Settle an Estate in FL (5E)	$26.95
____	1-57248-339-3	How to Start a Business in FL (7E)	$21.95
____	1-57248-204-4	How to Win in Small Claims Court in FL (7E)	$18.95
____	1-57248-381-4	Land Trusts in Florida (7E)	$29.95
____	1-57248-338-5	Landlords' Rights and Duties in FL (9E)	$22.95
		GEORGIA TITLES	
____	1-57248-340-7	How to File for Divorce in GA (5E)	$21.95
____	1-57248-180-3	How to Make a GA Will (4E)	$16.95
____	1-57248-341-5	How to Start a Business in Georgia (3E)	$21.95
		ILLINOIS TITLES	
____	1-57248-244-3	Child Custody, Visitation, and Support in IL	$24.95
____	1-57248-206-0	How to File for Divorce in IL (3E)	$24.95
____	1-57248-170-6	How to Make an IL Will (3E)	$16.95
____	1-57248-247-8	How to Start a Business in IL (3E)	$21.95
____	1-57248-252-4	The Landlord's Legal Guide in IL	$24.95
		MARYLAND, VIRGINIA AND THE DISTRICT OF COLUMBIA	
____	1-57248-240-0	How to File for Divorce in MD, VA and DC	$28.95
____	1-57248-359-8	How to Start a Business in MD, VA or DC	$21.95
		MASSACHUSETTS TITLES	
____	1-57248-128-5	How to File for Divorce in MA (3E)	$24.95
____	1-57248-115-3	How to Form a Corporation in MA	$24.95
____	1-57248-108-0	How to Make a MA Will (2E)	$16.95
____	1-57248-248-6	How to Start a Business in MA (3E)	$21.95
____	1-57248-398-9	The Landlord's Legal Guide in MA (2E)	$24.95
		MICHIGAN TITLES	
____	1-57248-215-X	How to File for Divorce in MI (3E)	$24.95
____	1-57248-182-X	How to Make a MI Will (3E)	$16.95
____	1-57248-183-8	How to Start a Business in MI (3E)	$18.95
		MINNESOTA TITLES	
____	1-57248-142-0	How to File for Divorce in MN	$21.95
____	1-57248-179-X	How to Form a Corporation in MN	$24.95
____	1-57248-178-1	How to Make a MN Will (2E)	$16.95
		NEW JERSEY TITLES	
____	1-57248-239-7	How to File for Divorce in NJ	$24.95
____	1-57248-448-9	How to Start a Business in NJ	$21.95

Qty	ISBN	Title	Ret
		NEW YORK TITLES	
____	1-57248-193-5	Child Custody, Visitation and Support in NY	$26.9
____	1-57248-351-2	File for Divorce in NY	$26.9
____	1-57248-249-4	How to Form a Corporation in NY (2E)	$24.9
____	1-57248-401-2	How to Make a NY Will (3E)	$16.9
____	1-57248-199-4	How to Start a Business in NY (2E)	$18.
____	1-57248-198-6	How to Win in Small Claims Court in NY (2E)	$18.9
____	1-57248-197-8	Landlords' Legal Guide in NY	$24.9
____	1-57071-188-7	New York Power of Attorney Handbook	$19.
____	1-57248-122-6	Tenants' Rights in NY	$21.
		NORTH CAROLINA AND SOUTH CAROLINA TITLES	
____	1-57248-185-4	How to File for Divorce in NC (3E)	$22.
____	1-57248-129-3	How to Make a NC Will (3E)	$16.
____	1-57248-371-7	How to Start a Business in NC or SC	$24.
____	1-57248-091-2	Landlords' Rights & Duties in NC	$21.
		OHIO TITLES	
____	1-57248-190-0	How to File for Divorce in OH (2E)	$24.
____	1-57248-174-9	How to Form a Corporation in OH	$24.
____	1-57248-173-0	How to Make an OH Will	$16.
		PENNSYLVANIA TITLES	
____	1-57248-242-7	Child Custody, Visitation and Support in PA	$26
____	1-57248-211-7	How to File for Divorce in PA (3E)	$26
____	1-57248-358-X	How to Form a Corporation in PA	$24
____	1-57248-094-7	How to Make a PA Will (2E)	$16
____	1-57248-357-1	How to Start a Business in PA (3E)	$21
____	1-57248-245-1	The Landlord's Legal Guide in PA	$24
		TEXAS TITLES	
____	1-57248-171-4	Child Custody, Visitation, and Support in TX	$22
____	1-57248-399-7	How to File for Divorce in TX (4E)	$24
____	1-57248-114-5	How to Form a Corporation in TX (2E)	$24
____	1-57248-255-9	How to Make a TX Will (3E)	$16
____	1-57248-214-1	How to Probate and Settle an Estate in TX (3E)	$26
____	1-57248-228-1	How to Start a Business in TX (3E)	$1
____	1-57248-111-0	How to Win in Small Claims Court in TX (2E)	$1
____	1-57248-355-5	The Landlord's Legal Guide in TX	$24

SubTotal This page ____

SubTotal previous page ____

Shipping — $5.00 for 1st book, $1.00 each additional ____

Illinois residents add 6.75% sales tax ____

Connecticut residents add 6.00% sales tax ____

Total ____